Traded

Options

Simplified

Books by the same author

Stocks and Shares Simplified

Traded Options Simplified

Brian J. Millard

Copyright 1989 by Qudos Publications

All rights reserved

No part of this book may be reproduced or transmitted by any means without the written permission of the publisher.

ISBN 1 871857 00 7

Published by:

QUDOS PUBLICATIONS
16 Queensgate
Bramhall,
Cheshire SK7 1JT

Printed by E. Moore & Co. Ltd., Manchester

Contents

Preface	vii
1. Risk and the Stock Market	1
2. Technical terms in the Traded Options Market	13
3. Technical Indicators 1. Moving Averages	19
4. Technical Indicators 2. Channel Analysis	39
5. Relationship between Share and Option Prices	57
6. Option Strategies	83
7. Buying Call Options	89
8. Writing Call Options	109
9. Buying Put Options	125
10. Writing Put Options	141
11. Advanced Strategies 1. Spreads	153
12. Advanced Strategies 2. Straddles and Combinations	173
Appendix	179

Preface

In spite of the great success of the privatisation issues over the last few years, the average private investor steers well clear of the Traded Options market. There are several reasons for this, such as a feeling that traded options are an extremely risky area of investment, and that in any case they are so complex that they are too difficult for the average investor to understand.

This book is intended to remove these misconceptions about traded options. It is shown that far from being extremely risky, the proper application of logical methods can make Traded Options a safer vehicle for profit than a straightforward investment in shares. The same logical methods make the selection of the correct traded option for the particular investment circumstances hardly any more difficult than the selection of the correct share.

As a well prepared traded options investor, you will laugh as the market rises, smile as it falls, and chuckle as it stays within a narrow range, because you will be able to take a profitable stance whatever the market is doing.

February 1989   Brian J. Millard
                                                    Bramhall

CHAPTER 1

Risk and the Stock Market

Prior to the crash of 1987, those investors taking part in the Government's privatisation of TSB, British Gas, Rolls-Royce, etc. might have thought that money could be made for the asking in the stock market. The reason these, and indeed any other investor bought shares is because they anticipated that they would achieve a better return on their capital by this method than by leaving their money on deposit. However, since the crash, an air of realism now prevails, and investors accept the fact that there is a higher degree of risk associated with investment in the stock market than there is with investment in say a bank deposit account or a building society. Investors therefore have some understanding of the relationship between risk and return, which can be stated quite simply as "the higher the return, the higher the risk".

Outside the common factor that they wish to make a profit from their investments, investors are a very diverse set of people with many different ideas about how much profit can be achieved and how they can go about making this profit. Some will be perfectly satisfied if they do slightly better than if they had put their money into a building society, while others have very much higher expectations, say of perhaps doubling their money within a couple of years. Some investors will take the view that once made, an investment should be left to mature for a number of years, since the underlying trend of the stock market has been rising for nearly twenty years, and therefore a profit becomes inevitable. Others prefer a more active approach, buying and selling at frequent intervals, taking advantage of short term fluctuations in the market. The first type of investor is, by and large, exposing himself to less risk than the second type of investor.

MINIMISING THE RISK

As applied to the stock market, the concept of risk would appear to imply that there are "good" shares and "bad" shares, but one of the most successful amateur investors ever on the New York Exchange, Nicholas Darvas, restates this quite admirably: there are only rising shares and falling shares. Since a rising share will not rise forever, and a falling share has a floor of zero, nothing is surer than that rising shares will turn into falling shares, while falling shares,

2 TRADED OPTIONS SIMPLIFIED

except for those thankfully rare cases where the company goes out of business, will turn into rising shares. This vision of the stock market now helps to clarify our ideas of risk as being dependent on how far along an existing upward or downward trend the particular share is at the point in time at which an investment in that share is contemplated. Risk should be minimal when a share begins to rise after a fall, and maximal when a share begins to fall following a rise. Quite obviously the major component of risk can be seen to be the timing of the investment.

These periods of high and low risk are best illustrated by reference to a market index such as the FT Index. Points at which the Index itself begins to turn up (as indicated by for example a moving average) after a fall show periods

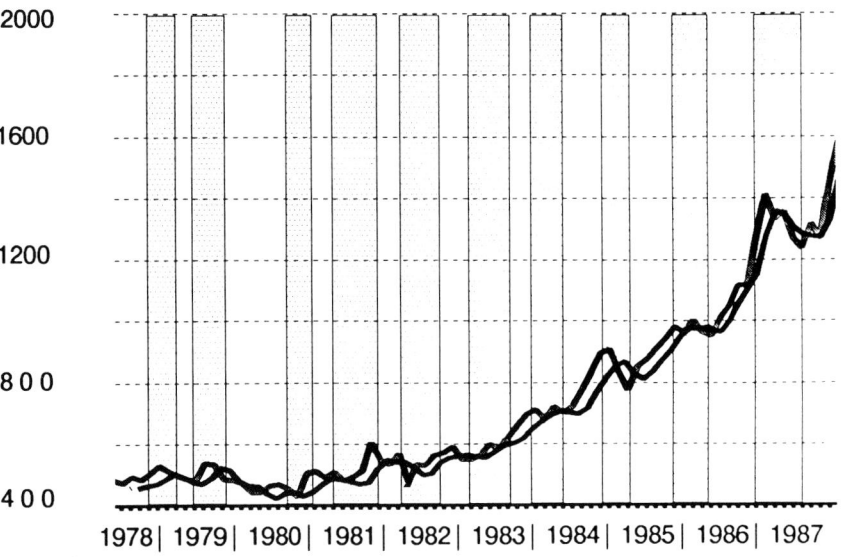

Figure 1.1. The FT Index (mottled line) and 13-week average (solid line) illustrating periods of high and low risk over the last 10 years. Periods of high risk are shaded, while periods of low risk are white.

of low risk in the market in general, and therefore, by implication, a period of low risk for purchasing particular shares. Conversely, when the Index begins to turn down after a rise (again using perhaps a moving average as the indicator), a period of high risk for purchase is being entered. These periods are shown graphically in Figure 1.1 for the FT Index, using the 13-week moving average as an indicator of market turning points.

Naturally, the key to determining these periods of low and high risk lies in developing good indicators of market turning points, and much effort has been expended by many analysts, including this author, on this problem. This aspect is discussed in a later chapter.

MAXIMISING THE RETURN

The return on an investment can be defined in a number of ways. We have to compare the value of the investment at some point with the original amount invested in that asset, in addition taking into account any dividends that may have been generated during the holding period. A simple definition, adequate for our purposes would then be:

$$\text{RETURN} = \frac{\text{ending value - starting value + dividends}}{\text{starting value}} \times 100\%$$

With this definition, it is of course possible to have negative returns, so that in the case of a total loss and no dividend payments:

$$\text{RETURN} = \frac{0 - \text{starting value} + 0}{\text{starting value}} \times 100\% = -100\%$$

There is still something missing from this definition, and that is the length of time over which the return has been calculated. Without this time period, a share which doubles in value in six months would appear to give the same return as a share which took ten years to do the same. Since this is patently not acceptable in terms of our investment philosophy, we should relate all returns to the same time period, in order that we will be able to compare the returns of two different investments.

We have a number of time periods to choose from, each of which can be defended as a logical choice depending upon one's personal investment characteristics. A one year period has some logic because interest rates are quoted as "per annum". A six month period has lesser logic although dividends are usually paid six monthly. A quarterly period is more appropriate for US investors because dividends there tend to be paid quarterly. However, the maximum timespan of nine months available in the traded options market precludes these longer time periods, and many investments in options may be for much shorter periods of weeks and sometimes days. Because of this, the most sensible standard time period for computing return on an investment will be taken to be the week. We can now define a weekly return (WR) as being:

$$\text{WEEKLY RETURN (WR)} = \frac{\text{ending value - starting value + dividends}}{\text{starting value x number of weeks invested}} \times 100\%$$

Note: in the case of traded options, there is no dividend payment unless the option has been exercised into the underlying security before the latter becomes ex-dividend.

Strictly speaking, the WR calculation should also take into account the costs involved in the transaction, but the difficulty in doing this is that costs may vary from one broker to another, and costs will also vary with the number of contracts taken (Chapter 2). Since we cannot therefore arrive at a consistent value, this will be left out of WR calculations, although where possible an indication of the costs involved will be given.

We can now see quite clearly from this definition of WR that high WRs are obtained either from a large increase in the value of the investment over some medium term, or a smaller increase in the value over a shorter term. The highest WRs are obviously obtained by a fortuitous combination of a large increase over a short time period.

This rather lengthy preamble to the question of investment return is necessary to clear the way to the important statement: volatile shares give the highest weekly returns. The simplest way of choosing volatile shares was discussed in Stocks and Shares Simplified, and amounted to selecting those shares with the highest ratio of high to low value in the yearly high/low column in those newspapers with a good coverage of daily share prices. As far as the London Traded Options are concerned, volatility is one of the criteria used in selecting the growing number of shares for which traded options are available. It is of interest to state the other criteria used, since they involve the aspect of safety of the underlying shares. During the five years prior to the introduction of option trading, the company must not have defaulted on the payment of interest, dividend or sinking fund instalment, or committed any breach of borrowing limitation. The company should also have a substantial market capitalisation, and there must be at least 10,000 equity shareholders.

It is useful to compile for the shares for which traded options are available, a volatility table of the ratio of yearly high to low value. This is done in Table

Table 1.1. High/Low Ratio During Previous Year for Traded Options Shares in August 1985, 1986 and 1987.

Share Hi/Lo:	3/8/85	2/8/86	1/8/87	Share Hi/Lo:	3/8/85	2/8/86	1/8/87
Allied Lyons	1.509	1.440	1.485	Brit & Comm	1.316	1.529	1.992
BP	1.211	1.144	1.747	Britoil	1.262	2.059	2.204
Cons Gold	1.200	1.312	2.160	Courtaulds	1.319	1.649	1.736
Comm Union	1.340	1.456	1.444	Cable & Wireless	1.348	1.299	1.346
GEC	1.410	1.400	1.364	Grand Met	1.191	1.295	1.378
ICI	1.343	1.409	1.518	Land Secs	1.219	1.243	1.782
M & S	1.304	1.359	1.558	Shell	1.232	1.222	1.548
Trafalgar House	1.175	1.384	1.609	Woolworth	1.657	2.100	1.355
Bass	1.222	1.344	1.440	GKN	1.278	1.486	1.595
Jaguar	1.531	1.746	1.229	Barclays	1.261	1.360	1.353
Midland Bank	1.238	1.421	1.243	Brit Aerospace	1.430	1.439	1.350
BAT	1.331	1.387	1.493	British Telecom	1.435	1.544	1.612
Cadbury Schweppe	1.239	1.333	1.545	Guinness	1.262	1.274	1.473
Ladbroke	1.177	1.246	1.562	LASMO	1.575	2.761	2.447
P&O	1.358	1.337	1.483	Plessey	1.827	1.500	1.465
Prudential	1.461	1.327	1.399	Racal	2.322	1.500	1.586
RTZ	1.285	1.539	1.995	Vaal Reefs	1.640	1.878	1.773
Amstrad	1.343	3.616	1.744	Beecham	1.300	1.378	1.347
Boots	1.240	1.271	1.438	BTR	1.311	1.369	1.348
Blue Circle	1.200	1.356	1.728	De Beers	1.380	1.689	1.859
Dixons	1.436	2.004	1.398	Glaxo	1.232	1.488	1.761
Hanson	1.313	1.340	1.436	Lonrho	1.194	1.489	1.376
Sears	1.294	1.427	1.551	Tesco	1.690	1.417	1.595
Thorn EMI	1.613	1.400	1.773	THF	1.352	1.424	1.567

1.1, the ratio being calculated at the first Friday in August for each of the years 1985, 1986 and 1987. One feature of this Table is that there is a measure of consistency, i.e. of the twelve most volatile shares in 1985, half of these featured among the twelve most volatile in 1986. Again, half of the top twelve in 1986 were also in the top twelve for 1987. As a rough rule of thumb, therefore, there is a good chance that a share which has exhibited high volatility in a particular year will continue to do so. This can be useful as an aid to deciding between two possible options where in other respects of timing, etc., there appears to be little to choose between them.

6 TRADED OPTIONS SIMPLIFIED

RISK AND RETURN

Although we have stated that volatile shares give the highest weekly returns, we should be quite clear that volatile shares can also give the highest losses, i.e. the lowest weekly returns. Therefore, in the absence of correct timing of the investment, there is a greater risk associated with investment in volatile shares than with their less volatile counterparts.

The simplest starting point is to assume an investment made in an average share from all the shares available in the U.K. stock market, and made at some random point in time, i.e. with no reference made to the high or low state of the market in general or the low or high state of the particular share price at

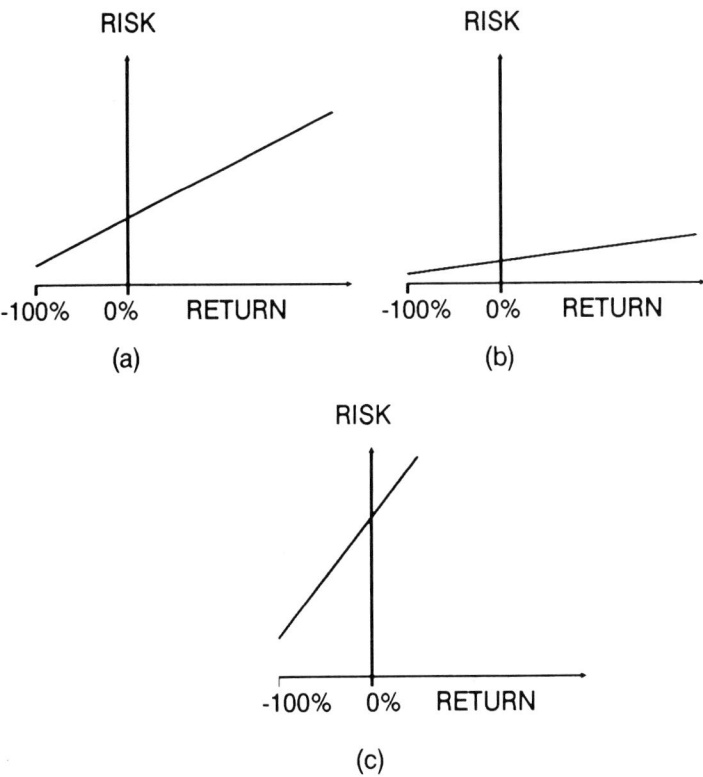

Figure 1.2. Risk-Return relationships (a) Average case (b) Volatile case with good timing of investment (c) Volatile case with bad timing of investment.

the time of the investment. A graph of risk versus return may then look like that shown in Figure 1.2(a). Except for one point on this graph, no attempt is made to put any values on either of the axes. The object is simply to illustrate a few points which can then be carried forward through this analysis.

The first point to make is that the return may be either negative or positive, i.e. we may lose some capital or gain some capital. The most negative return would be -100%, which of course represents the point at which we lose all our money. There is no maximum value on the most positive return, since this may, in fortunate circumstances rise to many thousands of percent.

The second point to make is that however small we would like it to be, there is still some chance of a total loss, so any stock market investment graph never starts from a point of zero risk, but from some small positive value.

Since Figure 1.2(a) typifies the risk/return relationship for an average share rather than a particularly volatile one, then we can compare this with two other cases - one where we have selected a volatile share and have achieved superior timing of the buying decision, and one in which the timing is disastrously wrong. Figures 1.2(b) and (c) show these two other situations. Where the timing is good, as in Figure 1.2(b), then the risk associated with a particular return is much lower than for the average case. It should be seen quite clearly from the Figure that the risk of total loss (-100% return) or of zero gain is considerably less than in the average case (Figure 1.2(a)). Where the timing is bad, as in Figure 1.2(c) then the risk associated with a particular return is higher than in the average case, and very much higher than when the timing is good. This is also very obvious for the total loss and the zero gain points on the graph. Clearly, investors are always looking for a situation in which the risk is minimised while the return is maximised, i.e. to approach the position shown in Figure 1.2(b), but naturally this state of affairs is difficult to achieve.

The main components of risk and return are the volatility of the particular share price and the timing of the investment. Readers of Stocks and Shares Simplified will be aware that this author's view is that investment should take place in volatile shares. These are easy to find since all one has to do is to compose a list of shares in decreasing value of the ratio of the high to the low price for the past year or major portion of the year. The main way in which risk can be decreased then lies in the selection of the correct buying and selling times. There will be periods during which buying shares will be highly risky, and periods when buying shares is less risky. This was shown for the FT Index in Figure 1.1.

The author's view of the market is that the most important decision an investor has to take is When? The What? decision, although important, is of secondary importance. The market itself dictates when to buy and when to sell at levels of acceptable risk. Investors who step out of synchronisation with the market do not increase their possibility of a high return. They simply increase the risk associated with that return. As long as this fact is realised, then it is perfectly acceptable for them to yield to pressure from brokers, bank managers, investment newsletters, etc. to make investments at times other than market lows and to sell at times other than market highs.

Chapters 3 and 4 of this book examines in some detail ways of deciding the best buying and selling points in the market. The use of moving averages as indicators of market turning points has already been covered extensively in 'Stocks and Shares Simplified'. Readers of that book will also have seen that longer term moving averages were used to try to predict the extent of future price movements. Since writing 'Stocks and Shares Simplified' I have become aware of the work of J.M. Hurst in the United States, and it has become obvious that we were both arriving at similar conclusions by two different routes. These two approaches have now been combined in what may be termed "Channel Analysis", and this gives the investor the most powerful methods ever devised for stock market prediction. These techniques are of vital importance in giving the investor not only a feeling for the direction which the market in a particular share is taking, i.e. upwards, downwards or sideways, but also some idea of the target area for which the market is headed. This last aspect will be essential in enabling the investor to categorise himself in terms of expectation, as discussed later.

WHY INVEST IN TRADED OPTIONS?

An investor who restricts his activities to the buying and selling of securities quoted on the major markets is operating under quite severe restraints. These can be summarised as:-

- Profits are made only if the share price rises.
- Buying and selling is limited to certain periods in the overall price cycle if risk is to be minimised.
- Moving outside such periods increases risk without a compensating increase in the return from the investment.
- Consideration of items 1 to 3 shows that an investor may have to spend months or even years out of the market if the latter is trending downwards.
- Typical returns from such investment average out somewhere in the range 10 - 50% on an annualised basis.

Of course, there have to be some positive aspects to this type of investment, some of which may be summarised as:

- A long term policy of buy and forget is often successful, thus suiting investors with little time to spend on management of their portfolios.
- Decisions on what to buy and when to buy are relatively simple if general guidelines are followed.
- The risk of total loss is quite small if an investor sticks with shares of say the top 100 companies.
- Generally speaking, the more time that is spent on studying the market, the greater will be the return.

The advantage of using traded options is that the investors achieve total flexibility in terms of timing, degreee of risk and the return on the investment. The following points can be compared with those made above:-

- Whatever the direction of the market, upwards, downwards or sideways, a profitable stance can be taken.
- A position can be taken at any time during the overall market cycle.
- The investor can choose the amount of risk appropriate to his psychology. In general the higher the risk the higher the return to the investor.
- The return on an investment can range up to many thousands of percent.

However, not all aspects of traded options are positive, and there are some disadvantages:-

- The longest timescale possible in the traded options market is nine months.
- There is a bewildering array of possibilities available, making decisions quite difficult to take.
- There is a substantial risk of total loss, even with options in giants such as ICI and British Telecom.

In view of these major advantages, we might ask why only a small proportion of those investors active in the stock market use traded options as part of their investment strategy. There are several reasons for this, one major reason being that traded options are perceived as being much riskier than normal investment in shares. Another reason is that traded options appear to be complicated to understand, requiring a great deal of specialised knowledge.

It is to be hoped that both of these difficulties will be rectified by this book. Certainly it will be seen that traded options, used correctly, can actually reduce the risk of investing in the stock market. Hopefully, this book will also aid the understanding of the subject so that investors will see that traded options form an invaluable part of the wider investment scene.

Finally, it is useful to show the trade-off between risk and return as exemplfied by two investors. One of these invests in a share, while the other invest in a call option. Both investors, naturally, expect a useful rise in the price of the share itself. At the beginning of December, the Commercial Union share price was 303p. The January 330 calls were selling at 10p. The "conservative" investor who bought shares saw them rise to 357p over the next two weeks.

Therefore

$$\text{Percentage gain} = \frac{357 - 303}{303} \times 100\% = 17.8\%$$

$$\text{The Annualised percentage gain} = \frac{17.8 \times 52}{2} \times 100\% = 462.8\%$$

The Weekly Return (WR) = 17.8/2 = 8.9%

These are of course very impressive returns when expressed as annualised percentage gains or weekly returns. However, compare these with those made by the investor in the call options at 10p. Within the two week period these had increased in value to 38p.

Therefore

$$\text{Percentage gain} = \frac{38 - 10}{10} \times 100\% = 280\%$$

$$\text{The annualised percentage gain} = \frac{280 \times 52}{2} \times 100\% = 7280\%$$

Since this gain of 280% in the call option premiums was made over a period of two weeks, it follows that:

Weekly Return (WR) = 280/2 = 140%

However we must not forget that the returns are only obtainable at the expense of a far greater risk in the case of options than with shares. Supposing, for example, the Commercial Union share price had fallen slowly over the next seven weeks, i.e. to the expiry date of the January options. If the price was then, for the sake of argument, 290p, then the loss to the investor in the shares is:

$$\text{Percentage loss} = \frac{290 - 303}{303} \times 100 = 4.3\%$$

Since this loss occurred over a period of seven weeks, then it follows that the annualised percentage loss is:

$$\frac{4.3 \times 52}{7} \times 100\% = 31.8\%$$

$$\text{The WR} = \frac{-4.3}{7} \times 100\% = -0.6\%$$

Compare this with the option position, which now expires worthless, since the striking price of 330p is higher than the share price of 290p at the option expiry time.

$$\text{Percentage loss} = \frac{0 - 10}{10} \times 100\% = 100\%$$

$$\text{The annualised percentage loss} = \frac{100 \times 52}{7} \times 100\% = 742.8\%$$

$$\text{The WR} = \frac{100}{7} \% = -14.2\%$$

This example clearly shows the trade-off between risk and return. Those investors who are seeking a higher return from their investment must of necessity tolerate a higher risk. Those investors who are uncomfortable with a high degree of risk can take a position where the risk is lower, but they will have to be satisfied with a lower return.

CHAPTER 2

Technical Terms in the Traded Options Market

Before we can enter into any meaningful discussion on traded options, it is necessary to define the numerous technical terms used so that these can be clearly understood.

Option: in particular a traded option, just like an ordinary share, is a marketable item involving buyers and sellers. In traded options jargon a seller is also called a "writer" of the traded option. On opposite sides of a traded options deal therefore we have a buyer and a writer. Options are of two types - call options and put options.

Call options: the buyer of a call option has the right to buy shares from the writer at an agreed price known as the exercise price or strike price.

Put options: the buyer of a put option has the right to sell shares to the writer at an agreed exercise price.

Option class: this means all the various options available in the shares of a particular company, taking into account puts, calls, exercise prices and expiry dates.

Option series: this means all the options in a class which share the same exercise price and expiry date. Examples are Boots March 200 series, Shell July 1000 series, etc.

Exercise (strike) price: this is the agreed price at which shares will be bought by the buyer from the writer of a call option if the buyer exercises the option. Similarly it is the price at which the shares will be sold by the buyer of a put option to the writer if the buyer exercises the option.

Expiry date: the date on which the option expires. Options have a maximum life of nine months.

Premium: the price which the buyer pays for the call or put option. This is the only aspect of the contract which can vary in price since it is subject to normal market forces.

Out-of-the-Money: these are call options where the share price is below the strike price, and put options where the share price is above the strike price.

At-the-Money: these are call options or put options where the share price is equal to the strike price.

In-the-Money: these are call options where the share price is above the strike price, and put options where the share price is below the strike price.

Consideration: the cost of the option based on the premium and number of contracts, but excluding commissions, VAT, etc.

Contract: one contract is the minimum unit which can be traded. A contract usually refers to an option on 1000 shares in the underlying security. There are exceptions to this however, and this unit can change as a result of rights issues, etc. When placing an order with a broker, do not mention the number of shares for which you are buying the option, but simply the number of contracts, from one contract upwards, i.e. for options on 5000 shares you would buy five contracts. Do not forget the mathematics, which in the case of five contracts for an option quoted as having a premium of say 20p would lead to a consideration of :

$$1000 \times 20p \times 5 = £1000$$

i.e.

(usual no. of shares/contract = 1000) x (premium = 20p) x (no. of contracts = 5)

Of course, the dealing costs are omitted from this calculation, but examples will be given later.

Expiry Dates and Exercise Prices: When a new option class is created, its expiry dates are assigned permanently into one of three available cycles. The first cycle has expiry dates of January, April, July and October, the second cycle expiry dates of February, May, August and November and the third cycle dates of March, June, September and December. The consequence of having such cycles is that for any option, there are always three different expiry dates available, with the maximum being nine months away from the date of introduction. The other two are then six months and three months in the

TECHNICAL TERMS   15

future. As time passes, these dates obviously come nearer, but when, three months from the introduction of the option the short term option naturally expires, it is replaced by a new option once again nine months in the future. The actual day of expiry in the particular month is usually the third or fourth Wednesday in the month, except for those occasions when the Exchange is closed for a bank holiday such as Christmas or Boxing Day. The buyer of options must take great care to be aware at all times of the impending expiry of an option, since decisions have to be taken regarding the fate of the options. Forgetting about the expiry of an option could be expensive. The three decisions available at all times during the life of an option are:

1. Sell the option at any time prior to the expiry date.

2. Exercise the option by buying the underlying security at the exercise price (call option) or selling the underlying security at the exercise price (put option).

3. Do nothing. Eventually the option expires. Naturally this course should only be taken where there is no advantage in exercising the option, i.e. when it has become worthless.

Just as expiry dates are decided by the traded options market authorities, so are the exercise prices. These prices will depend totally upon the underlying security price at the time the option is created. At that time, two exercise prices are created, one below and one above the security price. The difference between these two prices is usually about 10% of the share price, subject to the fact that the exercise prices are usually, but not always, rounded to say the nearest 10p.

The thinking behind traded options is to try to maintain the availability of exercise prices above and below the current security price. This means that as the price of the underlying security rises or falls outside of the current range of exercise prices, new ones will be introduced to maintain this situation. Such security price rises or falls can mean that a particular exercise price disappears from your newspaper. If this happens before the expiry date, it does not mean that the series ceases to exist, but that the newspaper does not wish to use too much space in its traded options listings. Of course a price movement the wrong way means that the option has become worthless, but a favourable price movement can convert your option into a pot of gold.

16 TRADED OPTIONS SIMPLIFIED

Dealing Costs: The costs involved in dealing in Traded Options are comprised of three components: broker's commission, a fee to the London Options Clearing House (LOCH) and the ubiquitous VAT. Broker's commission is also subdivided into a fixed charge per option contract plus an amount based on the level of option money involved. The fixed charge at present is £1.50 for each contract which is opened or closed. Broker's commission in the Traded Options market is subject to a minimum, but this differs from dealer to dealer. As a guide, the minimum commission is usually £20, although it may be possible to find brokers charging £15. Commissions are based on bands, the rate being 2.5% for the first £5,000 of Option money, 1.5% for the next £5000 of Option money and finally 1% on the excess Option money above this £10,000 level. Thus for brokers charging a £20 minimum, this minimum covers the two charge bands up to £10,000. Normally, if an option position is closed within five days of opening it, the broker will charge only the 1.50 per contract, waiving the percentage part of the commission. It is vital to understand how these dealing costs can eat into the profit margin, and normally an investor should be investing not less than £750 in order that these costs are kept down to a sensible level. This can be demonstrated from the following example:

1. Buy one contract of Racal February 200 calls @ 14p

		£
Option money = 1000 x 14p	=	140.00
Commission = 2.5% of 140	–	3.50
Fixed charge per contract	=	1.50
Total charges	=	5.00
Since these are below minimum,		
Minimum charge applied	=	20.00
LOCH clearing fee	=	1.50
VAT (15%)	=	3.22
TOTAL charges	=	24.72

When the option is sold, provided the gain is not so enormous as to take the option money from the sale to above £10,000 then the charges will be the same again. The total charges will therefore be £49.44. Based on one contract, where the option money is £140, a gain of more than 35% must be achieved in order to cover these charges.

TECHNICAL TERMS 17

2. Buy five contracts of Racal February 200 calls @ 14p

		£
Option money = 5 x 1000 x 14p	=	700.00
Commission = 2.5% of 700	=	17.50
Fixed charge per contract	=	1.50
Total charges	=	19.00
Since these are below minimum, minimum charge applied	=	20.00
LOCH clearing fee	=	1.50
Total	=	21.50
VAT @ 15%	=	3.22
TOTAL charges	=	4.72

Therefore we can see that the charges involved in buying and selling five Racal contracts are exactly the same as the charges involved in buying and selling one contract. In example 2, it will only be necessary to make a gain of just over 7% in order to cover these charges. Because of the minimum charge therefore, it is only above about £700-750 of option money that the charges come down to a tolerable level.

Payment for Traded Options: Note that unlike the buying and selling of normal shares, where all payments are at the end of the particular account, option payments have to be made by 10 am on the business day following the buying or selling of the option. Since this may be physically difficult in certain circumstances, the broker will probably ask for money to be paid into an account before you can start dealings. You cannot exercise an option on the same day as you purchase it because, under the above payment rule, you will not have paid for it until the next day.

Instructing Your Broker: Nowhere on the investment scene is there such an opportunity for confusion when instructing your broker than in the Traded Options market. It is absolutely vital that the correct form of words is used to convey your requirements. After all, in normal investment, you simply tell your broker whether you wish to buy or sell a certain share, and how many shares are involved. You may also wish to put a limit on the price you are prepared to pay. In Traded Options dealings you have to show whether you are opening or closing a position, the number of contracts involved, and the particular series, i.e. Allied Lyons April 300 calls. Thus to buy an option contract, you use the phrase "buy to open" and when you close that option at a later date you use the phrase "sell to close". One example would be "buy to open three contracts in Allied Lyons April 300 calls". To write an option contract you would say "sell to open" and state the particulars of the option you wish to write. It is important, because of the sometimes rapid movements in the market, that you arrange for your broker to call you back to inform you of the details of the bargain which has been struck on your behalf.

CHAPTER 3

Technical Indicators 1. Moving Averages.

This chapter will deal with the moving average method of determining the turning points in share prices. Readers of Stocks and Shares Simplified will of course be reasonably familiar with the concept of moving averages as indicators of buying and selling points, but will benefit from the somewhat different treatment that follows.

MOVING AVERAGES

1. Weekly Averages

(a) Medium and Long Term Averages

It can be seen by referring again to Figure 1.1 in Chapter 1, that the market, as indicated by the FT 30 Index, tends to move in waves over the course of time. These waves are not constant in either their distance apart (wavelength) or height (amplitude), but vary considerably. Moreover, there is present at any one time a confusing mixture of these waves. The object of the moving average approach is to use a simple mathematical treatment to sort out, from the complex mixture, waves of a duration that will prove to be useful in deciding when to buy and sell in the market. It is possible to some extent to visualise various wavelengths that are present by looking at the chart with your eyes screwed up. By doing this the fine detail of the weekly prices start to disappear, and the underlying trends become more apparent. The moving average approach is much more flexible, since by changing the number of weeks of the moving average calculation, waves of different wavelengths can be seen. Without going into mathematics deeply, the function of moving averages can be presented fairly clearly. Any average is of course calculated by adding together the items being averaged, and then dividing by the number of items involved. Thus a five week average is obtained by adding five consecutive weekly prices and dividing by five. The term "moving" is applied simply because this process of averaging is continued every week until there are no more weekly prices left, so the averaging process is moved along the weekly prices from the starting point, which may be years back in time, until the most

20 TRADED OPTIONS SIMPLIFIED

Table 3.1. Calculation of a 17-Week Moving Average for Racal

DATE	PRICE	SUBTRACT	17 WEEK TOTAL	17 WEEK AVERAGE
5 JUN 87	249.5	x	-	
12 JUN 87	265	x	-	
19 JUN 87	257	x	-	
26 JUN 87	275	x	-	
3 JUL 87	273	x	-	
10 JUL 87	277	x	-	
17 JUL 87	286	x	-	
24 JUL 87	281		-	
31 JUL 87	276		-	
7 AUG 87	265		-	
14 AUG 87	315		-	
21 AUG 87	312.5		-	
28 AUG 87	310		-	
4 SEP 87	308		-	
11 SEP 87	296		-	
18 SEP 87	304		-	
25 SEP 87	313		4863.0	286.0589
2 OCT 87	343		4956.5	291.5589
9 OCT 87	330		5012.5	295.3824
16 OCT 87	330		5094.5	299.6765
23 OCT 87	223		5042.5	296.6177
30 OCT 87	210		4979.5	292.9118
6 NOV 87	213		4915.5	289.1471
13 NOV 87	222		4851.5	285.3824

recent price has been used. Since the first five weekly values are used to calculate the first value of the five week average, which can be tabulated, as shown shortly, against the fifth week, it follows that we will end up with four less moving average values than we have number of weeks of prices. The number of weeks used in the average, such as five in the case just discussed, is known as the span of the average. If we choose some other span for the average, say 17 weeks instead of five, then the first average is tabulated against week 17, and we will end up with sixteen less average values than the number of weekly prices, and so on. As an example relevant to traded options, a calculation of such a moving average is shown for Racal Electronics in Table 3.1. The first 17 weeks' prices from 5th June 1987 to 25th September 1987 inclusively, add up to 4863, which is put in the 17-week total column. Dividing this by 17 gives 286.0589, which is the 17-week average entered in the last column. Although this process could be repeated by starting at the value for 12th June and adding the 17 values to 2nd October 1987, inclusively, this is not the simplest way to continue the calculation. It is far easier to take the current 17-week total, add in the next value, i.e. in the present example 343 on 2nd October and then subtract the value 18 weeks back from the new total, i.e. 249.5 for 5th June, thus giving the new 17-week total. By this method, you only have to add one number and subtract one number from the running total each week. It is useful to mark off with a tick in another column the week whose value has been subtracted. This is demonstrated in the example.

The effect of applying a moving average to any data is to remove, although not terribly efficiently, fluctuations with a periodicity equal to or shorter than the span of the average. In the case of stock market data, applying a 17-week average, for example, will reduce the contribution of all those waves or movements which have a periodicity, i.e. the time between successive peaks of 17 weeks or less. By the same token a 51-week average would only allow through much longer wavelengths, of greater than one year between successive peaks. Quite obviously, by careful selection of various spans of moving averages, the investor can focus on waves which (if they happen to be present) are appropriate to his frequency of buying and selling.

Some shares show much fewer dominant waves than others, and hence are useful for the purposes of illustrating what can be achieved by the use of moving averages. Since there are many thousands of shares available, it is sensible to select shares from these that fall into this similar category. Racal Electronics is such a share, and so for much of this Chapter the Racal share price is used to illustrate the effect of various moving averages.

In the following Figures 3.1 to 3.4, is shown the share price of Racal Electronics since 1983, and the effect of various moving averages, of 5 week, 17 week and 31 week spans. These are not magic numbers, but are used purely to illustrate various points. It will become obvious, as the discussion proceeds, how to select the span of the average best suited to the particular investment circumstances.

The share price itself shows several major peaks and troughs as well as the small ripples superimposed on these major waves. Thus there are peaks in the middle of 1983, end of 1984, middle of 1986 and past the middle of 1987 (the time of the big crash). There are corresponding troughs towards the end of

22 TRADED OPTIONS SIMPLIFIED

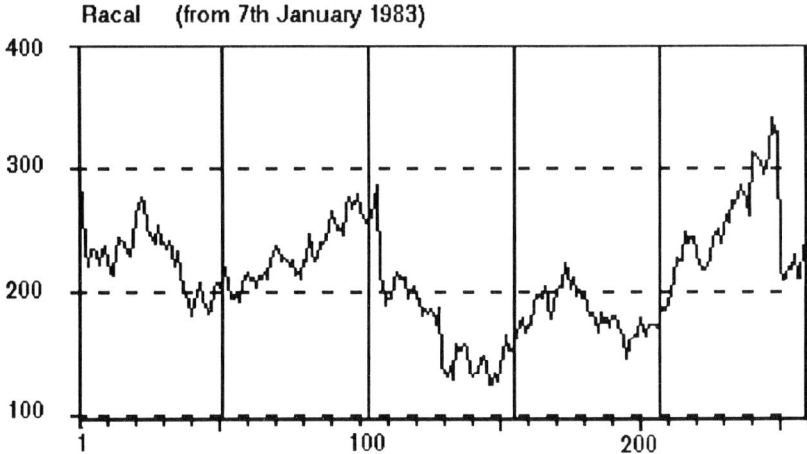

Figure 3.1. The Racal share price from 1983.

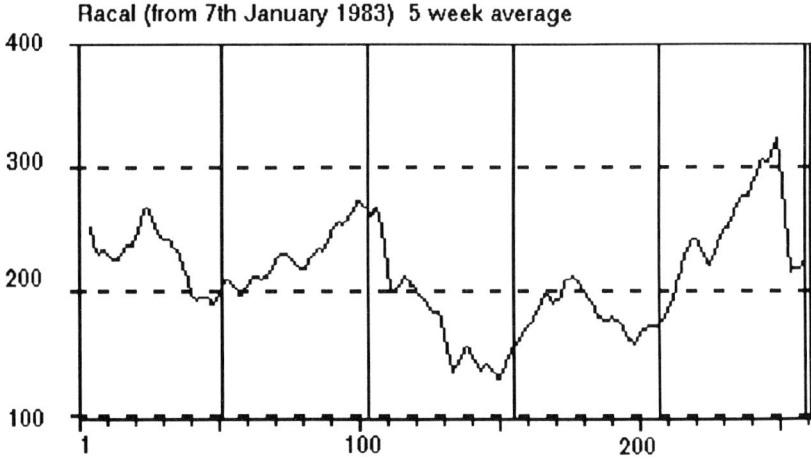

Figure 3.2. The 5-week moving average of the Racal share price.

1983, the middle of 1985 and the end of 1986. By screwing up your eyes these major waves, four in number, can be seen more clearly. A rough estimate shows the gap between the first pair and second pair of waves to be about one and a half years, and the gap between the third and fourth waves to be about one and a quarter years. Further inspection shows the periodicity of waves or

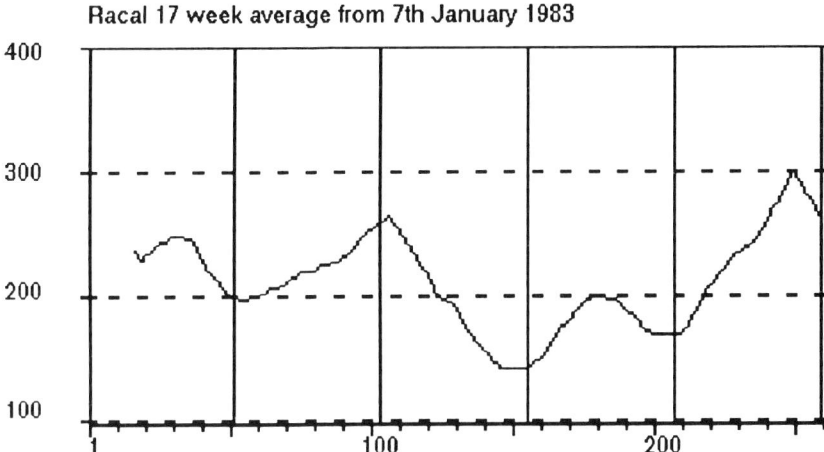

Figure 3.3. 17-week moving average of the Racal share price.

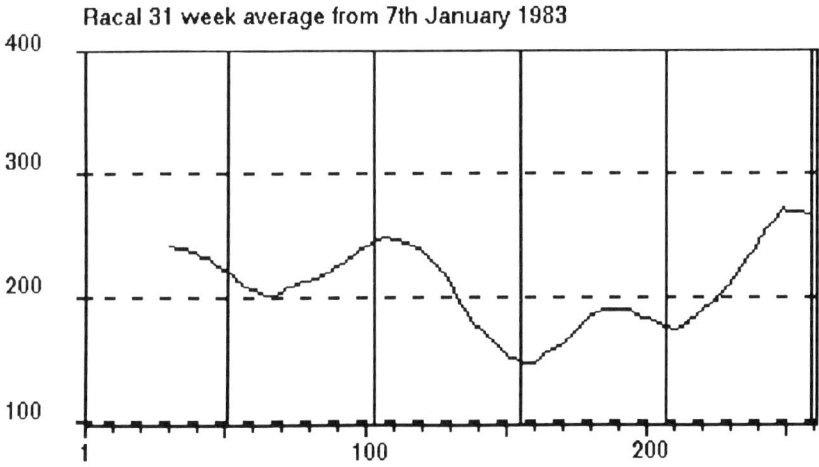

Figure 3.4. 31-week moving average of the Racal share price.

ripples of lesser duration to be very much shorter than these major waves, mostly being between say one week and twenty weeks. Bearing in mind what we have said about the periodicities allowed through by various moving averages, we can therefore expect, before actually carry out the calculation,

Table 3.2. 17-Week and 31-Week Moving Average Data for Racal

DATE	PRICE	17 WK AVGE	31 WK AVGE
4 APR 86	190	180.5882	162.4516
11 APR 86	204	183.4118	164.5806
18 APR 86	206	186.3529	166.9032
25 APR 86	206	189.2941	169.0968
2 MAY 86	224	192.4706	171.8700
19 MAY 86	218	194.9412	174.1935
16 MAY 86	204	196.3529	175.9355
23 MAY 86	212	198.8235	178.1935
30 MAY 86	200	200.2353	180.5161
6 JUN 86	204	201.8824	182.9677
13 JUN 86	196	202.2353	184.9032
20 JUN 86	200	202.2353	187.1613
27 JUN 86	190	201.6471	188.7097
4 JUL 86	184	200.9412	189.8065
11 JUL 86	186	199.7647	190.4516
18 JUL 86	178	198.9412	191.1613
25 JUL 86	170	198.3529	191.6129
1 AUG 86	186	198.1177	192.5806
8 AUG 86	178	196.5882	192.8387
15 AUG 86	180	195.0588	192.9677
22 AUG 86	174	193.1765	192.7742
29 AUG 86	182	190.7059	193.1613

that a five week average would still show these minor ripples, a 17-week average would have lost most of the minor ripples, and a longer term such as 31 weeks will show only the major waves. Note that in a case such as this, it is not necessary to move to 51-week or longer term averages to highlight the waves of 51 week or greater periodicity, because of the absence of any substantial wavelets of between 20 weeks and 51 weeks. This does not always hold true however, and where such is the case, much longer averages than 31-week may well have to be calculated. There is a very good reason for trying to get away with the smallest span possible, and that is because the gain in fidelity of longer averages is offset by the loss of data points as exemplified by the calculation of

MOVING AVERAGES   25

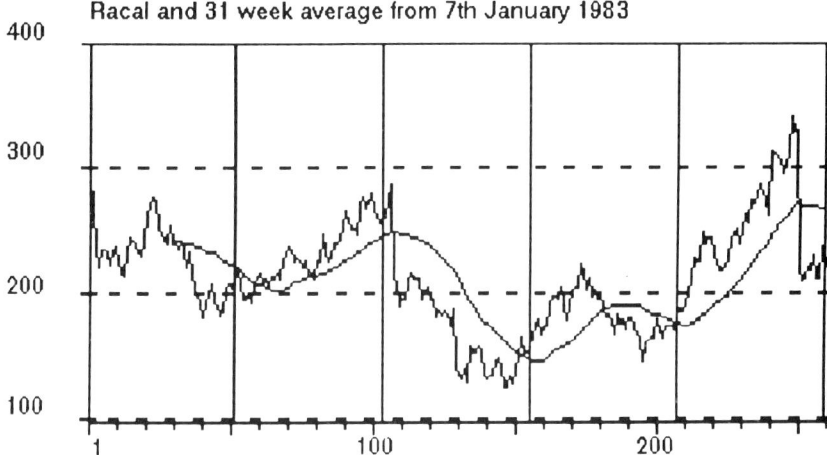

Figure 3.5. 31-week average superimposed on the Racal share price.

the 17-week average in which sixteen data points were lost. This also leads to unacceptable time lags before an average changes direction. These points are brought out in the discussion of the Figures.

Figure 3.2 shows the 5-week moving average of the Racal share price, and as expected, we retain a number of ripples superimposed upon the underlying waves. These ripples are, however, except for one in the middle of 1984 and one at the beginning of 1987, very minor in amplitude. It must be pointed out again that although share prices can move in common with each other, they also show a great deal of individuality. This is discussed later in the Chapter. Figure 3.3 shows the 17-week average of the Racal share price, and now the ripples with a periodicity of less than 18 weeks have been almost totally removed, giving a clear impression of the four large waves, even though the second and fourth have rather pointed tops. By applying a 31-week average, as shown in Figure 3.4, the waves now appear to much more rounded. Although the application of various moving averages, as shown in these Figures, is extremely valuable in highlighting the various waveforms present in share prices, we have not shown how they can be used as an aid to buying or selling of either shares or options. The simplest way in which they can be used is to determine turning points in the share prices. This is best illustrated by superimposing say the 31-week average upon the Racal share price, so that the relationship between these two can be more readily seen. This is done in Figure 3.5 for the same five year period that we have been discussing. The way in which the averages are presented on this chart shows that there is a time lag

26 TRADED OPTIONS SIMPLIFIED

between the jagged top of one of the major peaks in the share price and the corresponding top of the moving average peak. It will be shown shortly when the calculated data is given that this lag is one week more than one half of the span of the moving average, i.e. 9 weeks in the case of a 17-week average and 3 weeks in the case of a 5-week average. It becomes obvious that we can use the fact that an average has just passed its peak as an indication that the share price itself has just passed its peak, and therefore as a signal that the share should be sold. Conversely, when the average has just passed a trough we can use that fact as a signal that it is time to buy the particular share. Naturally this spotting of a peak or trough in the share price cannot be carried out on the share price itself because of the intermediate ripples in the price. Thus in the course of 1984, for example, there were five or six points at which the price appeared to have reached a peak, whereas the underlying trend was still upwards. Quite clearly therefore, a moving average is a fairly good indicator of the peaks and troughs in a share price, but as we can see from the example in Figure 3.5, there is a major disadvantage, and that is that the signal is given, in the case of a 31- week average, sixteen weeks after the price has peaked. We are faced with a dilemma here that we can reduce this time lag by shortening

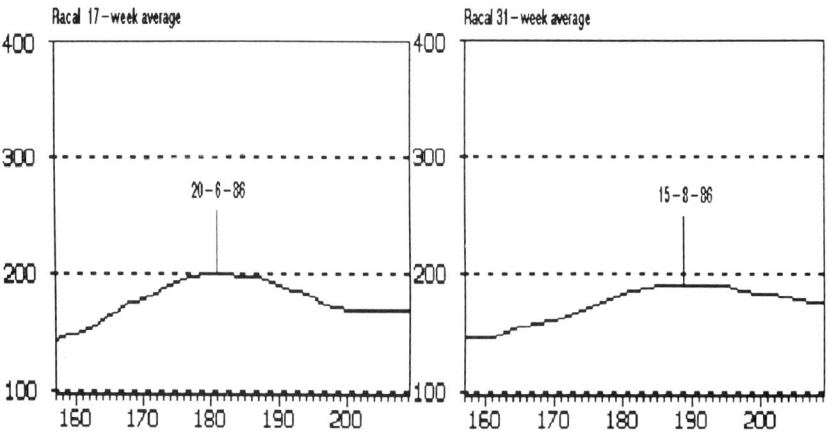

Figure 3.6. (a) 17-week average (b) 31-week average of the Racal share price. The 17-week average tops out 8 weeks before the 31-week average.

the span of the average, but, as can be seen from the 5-week average chart in Figure 3.2, we reach a stage where a number of false signals are give. Therefore we have to reach a compromise between the value of the average as an indicator and the delay in giving the signal. Obviously, with a long delay, the price has moved so far that there is no point in buying or selling, since most of the opportunity has been lost. The effect of these delays can be seen for the area of the chart around the high point in the middle of 1986 in Figure 3.6(a) and (b) where the 17-week and 31-week averages are plotted respectively. The high point of the share price itself, 224p occurred on 2nd May 1986. If the 17-week average had been used as the indicator of the turning point in the share price, then this topped out on 20th June, but of course this would not have become apparent until 27th June, when the average had fallen from its high point of the previous week. The delay in this case is therefore eight weeks, and the share price then was 190p. If the 31-week average was taken as an indicator, then this topped out on 15th August, which would not have become apparent until 22nd August. The delay in that case would have been 16 weeks, and the share price then was 174p. The penalty in this case for using a much longer average is therefore 16p, or about a further 9% drop in the share price. Naturally, if we had used a shorter average than 17-week, say 13-week, then the delay would have been shorter at six weeks, and the average would have given its signal on 13th June, when the share price was 196p. The numerical data for this time period is shown in Table 3.2.

It should be noted here that there is a difference in emphasis between someone who is investing in shares and someone who is investing in traded options. The investor in shares should be aiming to minimise risk at all times, even though this of necessity means that the profit in the buying and selling operation is reduced because the price has already moved some way in the direction of the trend before averages such as 13 or 17-week indicate a turn. On the other hand, except when using special strategies, the investor in traded options is operating at higher risk, and, more importantly, is relatively comfortable with this degree of risk. As well as this, the traded options investor operates on a much shorter trading cycle. Such an investor can therefore utilise averages of much shorter spans in order to reap the benefit of the increased gearing. The effect of the delays for 5, 13, 17 and 31-week moving averages on both the Racal share price and the November 200 puts is shown in Table 3.3.

This Table illustrates two points quite clearly. Firstly, options can move very quickly in the few weeks following the actual peak or trough in share price. In this example, the value of the put option has doubled between 2nd May and 30th May, when the five week moving average gave its signal. Secondly, the delay between the signals from a 31-week average and a 17-week average saw the share price fall by nearly 8%, but the put option became 40% more expensive. This shows how vital early timing is in the traded options market. In many cases it is necessary to collect daily price data and calculate very short term moving averages on this, for example 10 day and 20 day, but always bearing in mind that the shorter the average that is being used, the greater is the risk that the signal is false, and so one must be prepared to get out of a position very quickly if an adverse trend develops.

28 TRADED OPTIONS SIMPLIFIED

Table 3.3. Racal Share Prices and Premiums for November 200 Puts at Dates of Moving Average Signals.

Signal	Date	Share Price	November 200 Puts
Actual price peak	2 MAY 86	224	9
5 week average	30 MAY 86	200	18
13 week average	13 JUN 86	196	17
17 week average	27 JUN 86	190	20
31 week average	22 AUG 86	174	28

The minimum length of average which can be used while still retaining a situation where there would have been no false signals historically (a reasonable guide to lack of false signals in future) varies from share to share, and therefore has to be found by trial and error. One should always take the view that where a share price gives a disappointing result on a historical basis, then one can always find another one which behaves more properly.

There is a further point about the waves present in share prices which is relevant to the selection of a particular span for a moving average, and that is that the amplitude of a wave increases as its wavelength increases. This means that, in the case of the Racal Share price, the ripples of less than say 15 weeks duration have an amplitude of about 20p, while the major waves of more than a year's duration have amplitudes of between 50 and 100p. Therefore, if you can spot a share which has such a clear long term wave pattern as Racal, it is advantageous to use the longer term moving average which is necessary to highlight such a long wavelength and accept the greater time lag which this entails. There is one major proviso to this, and that is, as has been pointed out in the first Chapter, that the maximum life of a traded option is nine months. This means that the optimum wavelength which can be used would be that in which the time from the trough to the peak is nine months, i.e. a wavelength of eighteen months, since wavelengths are defined as the distance from one peak to the next.

(b) Short Term Price Movements

Moving averages as discussed above have, as explained, the property that they allow through the waves of longer periodicity than the span of the average, while waves of the same or shorter periodicity are attenuated. Because of this, we can only view short term movements as wavelets superimposed upon longer term waves. This can be seen from the Figure 3.2. where the 5-week average of Racal was presented. However, there is a way, involving an extra calculation, in which these short term movements can be isolated. Without going into the mathematics to any great extent, it is possible to attenuate the longer term variations and retain the short term movements. This is done simply by subtracting the moving average from the original price data. Before doing this, there is one important consideration, and that is that the data and the appropriate moving average are correctly aligned before subtraction is carried out. This requires a further explanation: mathematically, the average of a number of weekly prices has to be associated with the central week of the number of weeks taken. Virtually all books on the chartist approach to investment ignore this point, and just have we have done so far in this chapter, plot the average data as if it were associated with the last weekly price of the number of weeks taken. This is fine as long as only the fact that a moving average has changed direction is used as an indicator. How it is plotted is immaterial, since it is the latest numerical value that is being observed for a change in direction. We have used this approach so far to avoid having to explain why they would have been plotted half of their span back in time. However, the mathematical fact is that an average should be associated with the weekly value one less than half of the span back in time. Thus, in Table 3.1, the very first calculated point for the 17-week average should have been tabulated opposite week 9, i.e. eight weeks back opposite 31st July 1987 rather than opposite 25th September 1987. When such an average is plotted in this way, obviously the last plotted moving average point finishes this half of a span back in time, i.e. eight weeks back for a 17-week average. This point will not be laboured here for plotting of moving averages, since the object of this chapter has been to show how the various waves can be highlighted, and how the change in direction of the average signals a turning point for a particular wave. It will be important in the next chapter when the relationship between moving averages and share prices will be explored in much more detail. For the present, it is vital that the average is tabulated the correct half span back in time before the subtraction is carried out.

As an example, we can take the data in Table 3.1, where the 17- week average was calculated, and use it to give numerical data which can then be plotted to highlight those movements of a shorter periodicity than 17 weeks. These 24 prices have produced eight moving average values, and hence eight values for the difference. In order to see the short term movements in the Racal price, it is necessary to calculate a large number of these differences and then plot them. Note that unlike moving averages, which are always positive, the differences will fluctuate between positive and negative values. A plot of these differences from the 17-week moving average for Racal is shown in Figure 3.7.

The first impression is that there is very little regularity in the plot, and even where there is some regularity, this only lasts for a few months. This is indeed correct, and simply shows that Racal is not a good vehicle for investors who

30 TRADED OPTIONS SIMPLIFIED

Table 3.4. Calculation of a 17-Week Moving Average Difference for Racal

DATE	PRICE	SUBTRT	17 WK AVERGE	DIFFRNCE
5 JUN 87	249.5	x		-
12 JUN 87	265	x		-
19 JUN 87	257	x		-
26 JUN 87	275	x		-
3 JUL 87	273	x		-
10 JUL 87	277	x		-
17 JUL 87	286	x		-
24 JUL 87	281			-
31 JUL 87	276		286.0589	-10.0589
7 AUG 87	265		291.5589	-26.5589
14 AUG 87	315		295.3824	19.6176
21 AUG 87	312.5		299.6765	12.8235
28 AUG 87	310		296.6177	13.3823
4 SEP 87	308		292.9118	15.0882
11 SEP 87	296		289.1471	6.8529
18 SEP 87	304		285.3824	18.6176
25 SEP 87	313			
2 OCT 87	343			
9 OCT 87	330			
16 OCT 87	330			
23 OCT 87	223			
30 OCT 87	210			
6 NOV 87	213			
13 NOV 87	222			

are looking for predictable short term fluctuations. Contrast this with the same plot for the Plessey share over the same time period from 1983, where Figure 3.8 shows that we have much more regularity. This is much more clearly seen in the expanded chart shown in Figure 3.9, which gives a year of data starting from the end of 1984. Each difference value is now a discrete line, and the cyclicality is even more obvious if an envelope is drawn around these lines. The wavelength can be taken to be the distance in weeks from a point where the

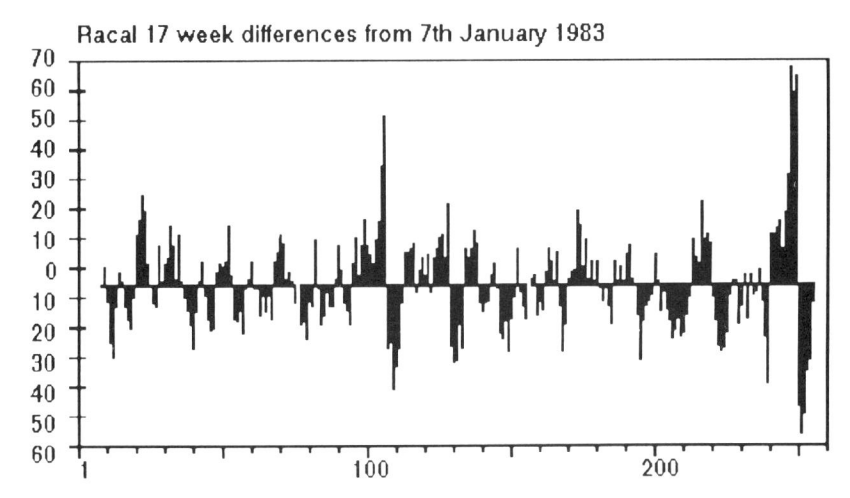

Racal 17 week differences from 7th January 1983

Figure 3.7. Differences between the Racal share price and the 17-week average.

difference crosses zero to the next point where it crosses zero going in the same direction. The successive wavelengths (the first one starts at week 100 and is obscured by the axis) are 15, 17, 18, 17 and 18. The average value of these is 17 weeks, and therefore we can state that, at least during 1985, there was present a short term fluctuation in the Plessey share price with a duration of 17 weeks. The amplitude of this fluctuation varied from a 30p down to about 10p. At this point, because the topic will be covered in depth in the next Chapter, we will just hint at the prospect held out by knowing the short term cyclicality of a share. This is that we can predict with an accuracy of a week or two, when such a cycle is starting on its upward or downward track. Provided that longer term waves are headed in the same direction, and this proviso cannot be stressed too highly, then there is a major opportunity to profit from investment in the correct traded option. The direction of the longer term waves is of course obvious from the charts of the longer term averages, as shown earlier, but the investor should be careful that such a longer term wave is not already too far along its cycle so that a reversal of direction is imminent.

2. Daily Averages

Obviously, weekly averages impose a limitation on the shortest movements that we can study. A three week average probably represents the shortest practical value for a weekly average, and in many circumstances there are fluctuations which are well defined and have shorter periodicity. In such cases,

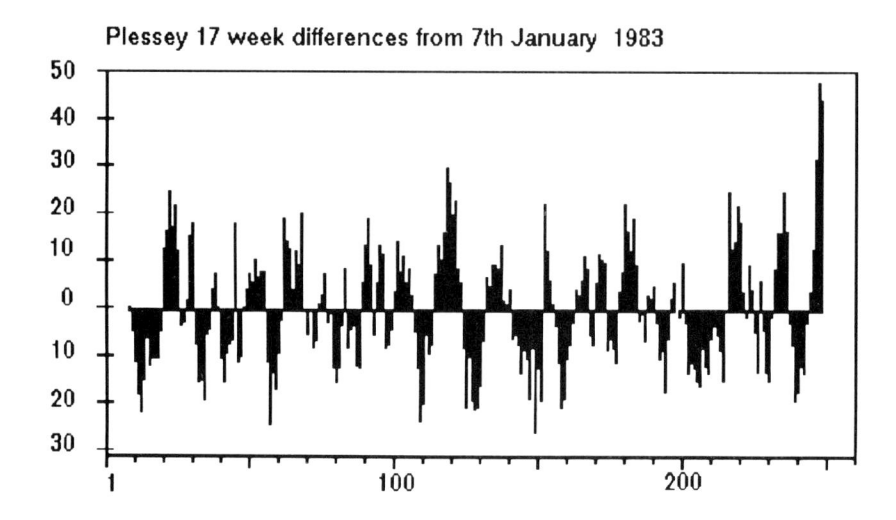

Plessey 17 week differences from 7th January 1983

Figure 3.8. The difference between the 17-week average and the Plessey share price.

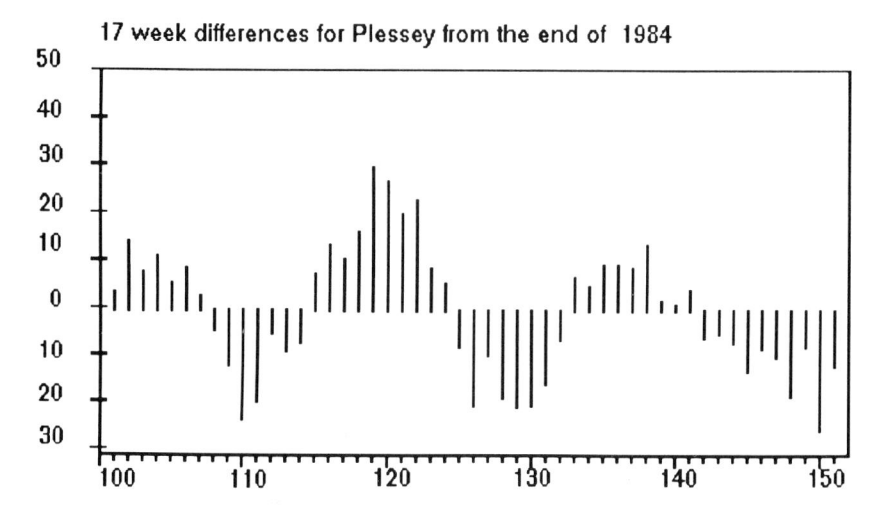

17 week differences for Plessey from the end of 1984

Figure 3.9. The difference between the 17-week average and the Plessey share price over the year from the end of 1984.

quite obviously, it is necessary to turn to daily data and daily averages in order to study these short term effects. Staying with Racal shares again, a daily plot and weekly plot over a fairly short time period can be used to illustrate the

MOVING AVERAGES   33

differences than can be seen from these two approaches. Figures 3.10(a) and (b) show the weekly data and daily data respectively for a twenty week period starting from August 3rd 1987. This period has been deliberately chosen as being one of the most turbulent in stock market history, covering Black Monday

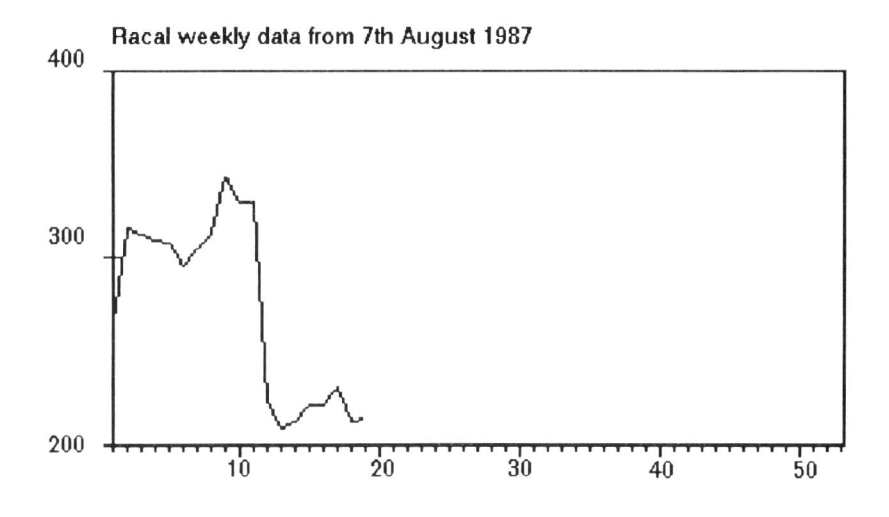

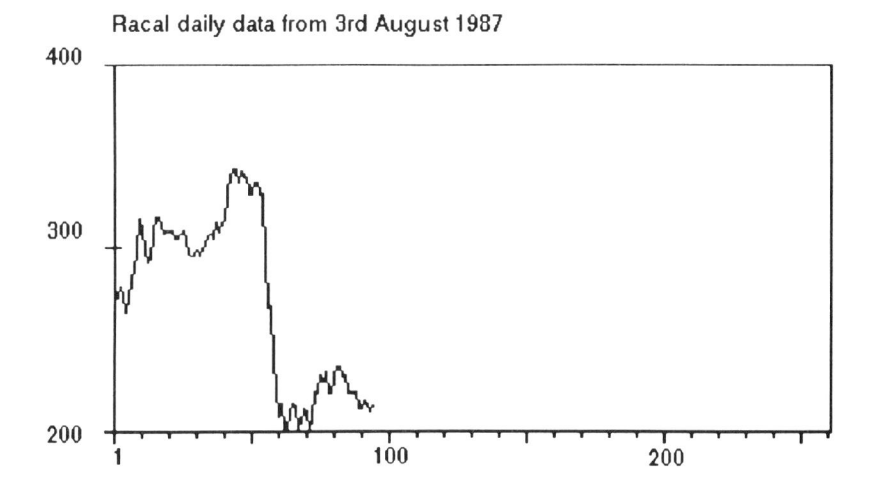

Figure 3.10. (a) weekly data (b) daily data for a 20 week period of the Racal share price from 3rd August 1987.

34 TRADED OPTIONS SIMPLIFIED

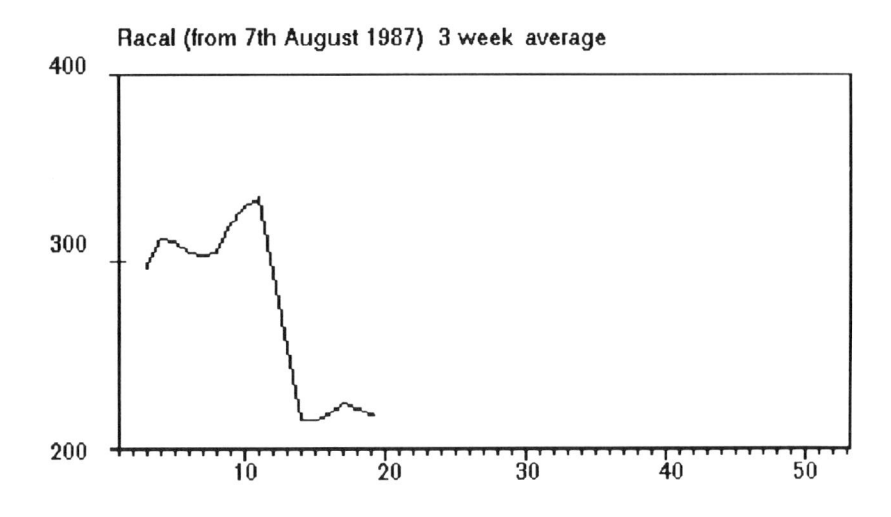

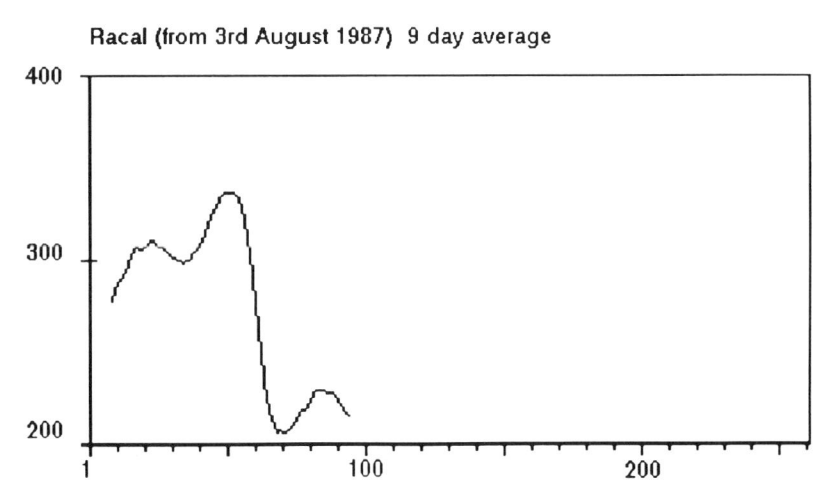

Figure 3.11. (a) 3-week average of Racal weekly data (b) 9-day average of Racal daily data over a 20 week period from 3rd August 1987.

when the market saw unprecedented falls in virtually every share price. The question here is whether any technical indicator, such as a moving average, is able to deal with such a rapid fall. The smallest waves that can be seen in the weekly data have wavelengths of 7 and 9 weeks. A number of smaller ripples are evident in the chart of the daily data. The amplitude of the waves of 7 and

MOVING AVERAGES   35

Table 3.5. Some Peaks and Troughs in Weekly Racal Data, with the Signals Given by a 3-Week Moving Average.

Date	Price	Comment	Date of Signal	Lag(weeks)	Price
14 AUG 87	315	peak	4 SEP 87	3	308
11 SEP 87	296	trough	25 SEP 87	2	313
2 OCT 87	343	peak	23 OCT 87	3	223
30 OCT 87	210	trough	2 NOV 87	3	221
27 NOV 87	231	peak	4 DEC 87	1	212.5

Table 3.6. The Same Peaks and Troughs in Daily Racal Data, with the Signals Given by a 9-Day Moving Average.

Date	Price	Comment	Date of Signal	Lag (days)	Price
14 AUG 87	315	peak	27 AUG 87	9	308
11 SEP 87	296	trough	21 SEP 87	6	307
1 OCT 87	343	peak	12 OCT 87	7	329
29 OCT 87	195	trough	6 NOV 87	6	213
24 NOV 87	236	peak	30 NOV 87	4	222

9 weeks duration is such that it is questionable whether, in view of the time lag for their moving average signals, a profit could be made out of them by normal investment in Racal shares. It is quite a different proposition as far as traded options are concerned, however, since the leverage gives quite respectable profit potential both in call and put options. In view of this, naturally the main concern is in how close to the peaks and troughs we can get with signals generated from the daily data and weekly data. As can be seen from Figures 3.11(a) and (b), the shortest span moving averages which give smooth enough curves are the three week average and the nine day average. The actual time lags for the peak and trough signals in the weekly data are given in Table 3.5. In the case of the daily data, there are are course a few more minor peaks and troughs observable compared with the weekly data, but to keep the comparison meaningful, only those peaks and troughs corresponding, to within a few days, of those shown in Table 3.5 are shown in Table 3.6.

The time lags in the daily data are of course business days, not calendar days, i.e. there are five business days to a stock market week. The advantage of using

36 TRADED OPTIONS SIMPLIFIED

Table 3.7. Price Rises and Falls Obtainable by Weekly and Daily Averages.

Comment	Differences: 3-Week Average	9-Day Average
peak 1 - trough 1	-5	+1
trough 1 - peak 2	-90	+22
peak 2 - trough 2	2	+116
trough 2 - peak 3	-8.5	+9

daily data and a daily moving average are immediately apparent from a comparison of these two Tables. The minimum time lag in the case of the daily data is 4 days and the maximum is 9 days. For the weekly data the minimum is 1 week and the maximum is three weeks. Since in traded options we can profit from falls as well as rises, an important measure of the usefulness of an indicator is the difference between successive peaks and troughs and successive troughs and peaks in terms of the price of the share at the time of the signal. The data in the Tables give three such differences, since there are three peaks and two troughs. The comparison between the weekly and daily differences is shown in Table 3.7.

Note that in the sense we wish to use them, all the differences should be positive, not negative numbers. A negative number implies that the price prevailing when a peak is indicated is less than the price prevailing when the corresponding succeeding trough is signalled. Conversely it also means that the prices prevailing for a trough is more than the price prevailing for the succeeding peak. Quite obviously these are situations where we would lose money. Table 3.7 shows clearly that a three week average is more than useless as an indicator for short term fluctuations, it is positively dangerous, whether used for share purchase or in traded options investment. On the other hand, the 9-day average gives positive results for all those fluctuations. Impressively, the 9-day average would have got you out with a 22p gain on the short term movement just before the Black Monday crash with a 22p rise. It must be noted here that this must not be taken as a general comment. A 9-day moving average would have got you out of a great many shares just before the crash, but it should be noted that this can only happen if the share, just as is the case with Racal, was already just past its peak. The majority of shares did not behave in this manner, and in these cases no indicator would have been useful. Philosophically, at least a proportion of one's investments would have been protected by the use of such a short term moving average. The question which arises now is whether such short term fluctuations, which obviously require moving averages of very short spans are of any use in normal investment in

Table 3.8. Behaviour of Racal Call Options During Two Share Price Rises.

DATE		OPTION	NOV	FEB	MAY
21	SEP 87	300	25	38	51
	(307p)	330	11	25	36
12	OCT 87	300	35(40%)	51(60%)	62(21%)
	(329p)	330	19(72%)	33(32%)	44 (22%)
6	NOV 87	220	22	33	
	(213p)				
30	NOV 87	220	22 (0%)	35(5%)	
	(222p)				

shares as opposed to traded options, and the answer has to be an unqualified No! Investment in shares depends upon a rise between a trough and the following peak, and in this example the first trough-to-peak rise was 22p and the second trough-to-peak rise was 9p. Based on a share price of around 300p, the first rise would leave very little after dealing costs, perhaps one or 2 percent, and the second rise would be totally swallowed up. The message must be that, with a few exceptions, short term movements with a periodicity of less than about six months are of no use to the investor in shares. The use of such short term variations in traded option investment is a quite different story, and can best be illustrated by the premiums on the various Racal call and put options prevailing at the times the signals were give.

Prior to the crash, a quite respectable profit could have been made from the small movement between 21st September and 12th October, of between 21% and 72%, depending upon which option had been selected. The other small movement between 6th and 30th November resulted in almost no movement of the 220 options, probably because the market was still suffering a hangover from the crash.

As could be expected, the crash provided a bonanza for anyone holding any kind of put option over the period of the crash. The prices on 6th November are educated guesses, on the conservative side, for the premiums pertaining to the 300 and 330 put options. They do serve to show the enormous gearing provided by options which lead to staggering gains when a large movement in share price occurs and you get it right. Thus a 35% drop in the share price becomes converted into a 2733% gain in the put option. Even the poorest gain in the various options available was still over 300%, i.e. the investment multiplied by a factor of four.

Table 3.9. Behaviour of Racal Put Options During Two Share Price Falls.

DATE	OPTION	NOV	FEB	MAY
27 AUG 87	300	17	25	27
(308p)	330	34	40	44
21 SEP 87	300	11(-35%)	20(-20%)	25(-7%)
(307p)	330	31(-9%)	37(-8%)	41 (7%-)
12 OCT 87	300	3	14	17
(329p)	330	15	25	30
6 NOV 87*	300	85(2733%)	100(614%)	115 (576%)
(213p)	330	105(600%)	115(360%)	130(333%)

* all values estimated due to non-availability of data

Naturally, gains of this magnitude of thousands or many hundreds of percent are not commonplace, but gains of a few hundreds of percent are. Such gains result from correct timing of market movements, using the techniques in this chapter and the next, plus the choice of the correct options, using the principles discussed in later chapters in this book.

CHAPTER 4

Technical Indicators - 2. Channel Analysis

Moving averages used in the way discussed in the last chapter are extremely valuable indicators of a change in the direction of an underlying trend in share prices. Of course, knowing that the trend has changed direction is only of value if the assumption is made that the share price will continue in its new direction for a long enough period to enable a profit to be made. This knowledge is gained from a study of the past history of the moving average of the particular span that one is interested in. Simple experiments with short, medium and long term averages can give an idea of the typical time for which trends continue. It will be noted of course that the longer the span of the average, the longer does that particular trend continue before changing direction, since the trends of lesser duration will have been filtered out (see Chapter 3). Viewing a moving average graphically tells us a great deal about how large or how small these trends are, and it is this that helps to put a brake on any euphoria we may have when a change in the direction of a trend is signalled. We are not able to tell with any great certainty just how long the trend will continue in its new direction.

The use of a moving average in isolation from the share price itself misses completely the valuable information that is available when a moving average and the share price are plotted on a chart at the same time. By this statement, we do not mean the widely used but mathematically incorrect practice of plotting the average with no time lag, and attaching great significance to those times where the price rises up through, or falls down below the moving average in question. We mean the powerful technique of channel analysis, which without question is the most accurate indicator of future price movements available to us.

CHANNEL ANALYSIS

When used properly, channel analysis will enable us to forecast points in the immediate future at which a trend is expected to change direction. Since our attention is focussed upon that point, even when we take into account the unavoidable uncertainties in stock market predictions, we will be able to recognise that the change in direction has occurred only a very short time after the event, unlike the time lags which we have to accept with a more simplified use of moving averages. This in itself makes channel analysis the most important technical indicator available. However, it has additional properties that make it particularly appropriate for use in traded options investment - subject once again to a degree of uncertainty, it can tell us the target area into which the price will move, and how long it will take to get there.

The basis of the method of channel analysis is the observation that, when correctly plotted, share prices oscillate about a moving average, and the oscillations can be contained within boundaries above and below the moving average. These boundaries constitute a channel. Thus share prices move within a channel, and moreover, it will be seen from the examples in the rest of this chapter that the channel is of constant width. This channel can be contructed by eye on a chart of the share price, or can be constructed about the moving average plotted on the chart. In the latter case of course a computer is of great value in carrying both the moving average calculation and the plotting function.

The increasing information which can be obtained from moving averages as we use them in different ways can be seen in Figure 4.1. Here we show in the upper panel the 17-week moving average for Racal plotted with the share prices themselves in the manner beloved of most technical analysts, i.e. with the moving average plotted up to date rather than half a span back in time. In the middle panel we show the average plotted in the mathematically correct manner, half of a span back in time, i.e. with a lag of 9 weeks. In the lower panel we show the upper and lower boundaries added, these boundaries being of such a width as to enclose most of the extremities of the price movements.

The only information that can be obtained from the upper chart is that the 17-week average has changed direction seven times during the time period covered by the chart. The longest leg of one of the trends is about one year, the shortest about half a year and that the average usually turns upwards or downwards about nine weeks after a trough or peak. As an indicator therefore, we can expect that a change in direction of the average signifies a new trend which started about nine weeks previously and which ought to last at least for six months. In the middle chart, the fact that the average is plotted half a span back in time now illustrates quite clearly the relationship between the price and the average. The price meanders about the average, but at points where the average is at a peak, the price has reached an even higher peak, and where the average has reached a trough, the price has reached an even lower level. These high or low points in the prices now coincide with high and low points in the average. The moving average now represents a "better" picture of the share price and where it is going, since the noise due to the short term variations is eliminated. Since we have a "better" picture of the way the share price is

CHANNEL ANALYSIS 41

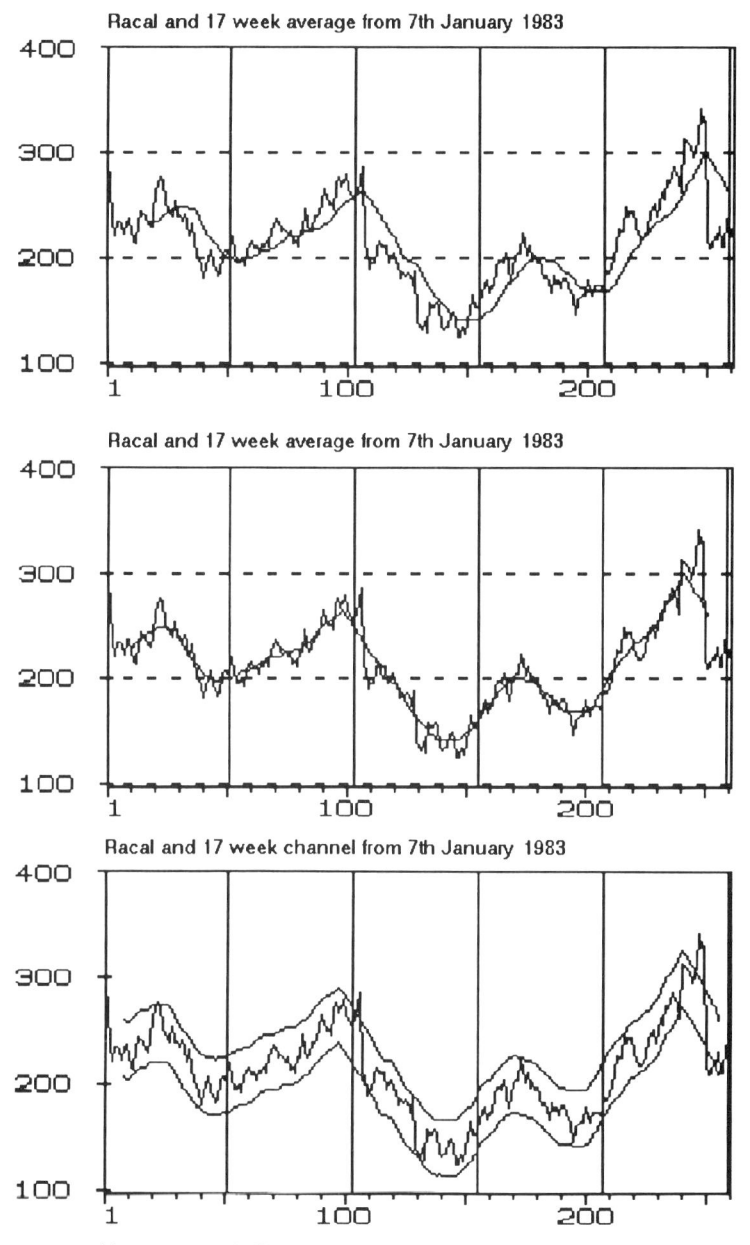

Figure 4.1. Upper panel: Racal share prices and 17-week average, no time lag. Middle panel: Racal share prices and 17-week average with time lag. Lower panel: Racal share price and 17-week channel.

behaving, we can much more readily predict where it is going in the future. Now if you examine more closely the way in which the price values themselves wander about the 17-week average, you will see that they never move too far away, and that it is easy to draw in the boundaries within which the price moves. This is done in the lower chart, and should now bring home quite clearly the value of this approach of channel analysis. In its simplest use, we can say that we can project the channel forward into the near future by drawing smooth continuations of the existing channel lines. Then when a price starts to draw close to either the higher or lower boundary, we should watch it carefully, since once it has touched or passed slightly through this level, a reversal of direction is expected. Note that although in this example we produced the channel by calculating the 17-week average, plotting it and drawing in the boundaries, it is perfectly easy and straightforward to do this without any calculation by drawing the smoothest two lines that will enclose most of the price movements, making sure that the vertical distance between the two lines is kept constant. You can take a photocopy of this page and try for yourself, or practice on any other chart that you have. It is useful to use either a flexible curve or the various curved stencils that are available from any good quality stationers in order to enable the smoothest channels to be drawn. In this simplest way therefore, channel analysis will enable us to improve our timing of a change in direction quite markedly.

Channels within Channels

So far we have discussed the drawing of just one channel, whether this is done by eye or by calculation of an average. As can be seen from the charts in Figure 4.1, this highlights waves with periodicities of one and two years. We know however from calculating much longer term averages on stock market data that there are waves of much longer periodicity than this, and these can be highlighted, providing we have data over a long enough period of time, by drawing the appropriate channel to encompass the channel we have already drawn. Again, just as with the first channel, we can either adopt the approach of calculating a longer term average, or simply draw in this second channel by eye. This channel is produced in Figure 4.2 from a calculation of a 75-week moving average, with the boundaries being drawn a constant amount above and below the average. For the sake of clarity, the average itself has been omitted, although naturally it will run down the exact centre of the channel. If we have enough data, we can continue in this way to draw further even longer term channels to enclose the existing ones.

You should be able to start to see now how these channels can be used to predict future price movements. When the share price approaches the inner channel boundary we expect it to reverse direction, and when the inner channel approaches the boundary of the next outer channel, again we expect the inner

CHANNEL ANALYSIS 43

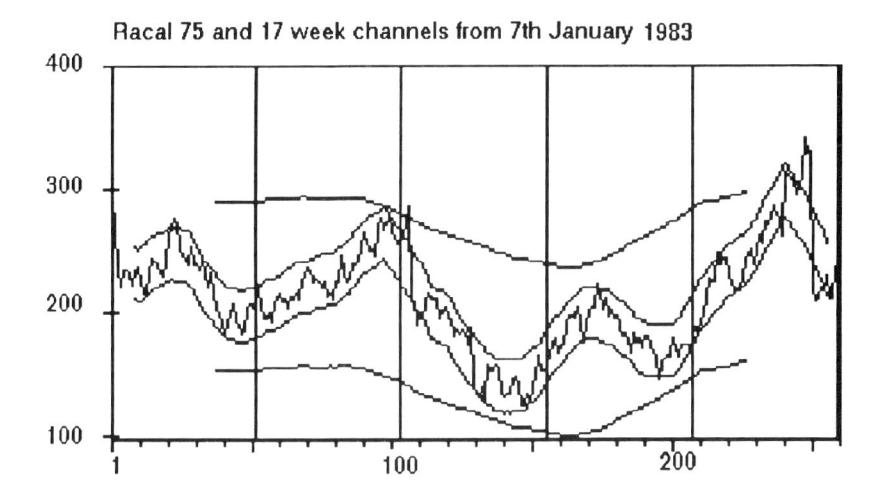

Racal 75 and 17 week channels from 7th January 1983

Figure 4.2. Racal 75-week channel enclosing the 17-week channel.

channel to reverse direction. We can extrapolate this process until we run out of channels. The key to prediction in the near future is of course the smooth extrapolation of the various channels into the future. When the channels are drawn by eye, or with the aid of a stencil, then naturally this projection into the future is part of the drawing process. If however the channels are drawn around the various calculated moving averages, then since the averages terminate half a span back in time, then so will the channels. In such a case there will be two parts to the extrapolation process, firstly to bring the channel up to the present time and secondly to project it into the future. Of course since the prices themselves continue to the present time, these serve as a useful guide in extending the channels to the present, from which point they can be extrapolated into the future.

It is useful to emphasise how we can determine various features as the share price history unfolds. For example, a minor trough in the weekly prices is only apparent a week after the event, i.e. when the price has moved up from the previous week's lower price. An intermediate trough is only apparent when the next minor trough to be seen does not descend as low. A major trough is only apparent when the next intermediate trough is at a higher level, and so on. These same arguments will apply to minor, intermediate and major peaks.

Thus:

- **minor troughs/peaks:** three successive weeks (days) prices in the correct relationship.
- **trough:** week (day) two lower than week (day) one and three.
- **peak:** week (day) two higher than week (day) one and three.
- **relevance to channels:** as many as possible of these minor troughs/peaks should touch boundaries of short term channels.

- **intermediate troughs/peaks:** three successive minor troughs/peaks in the correct relationship.
- **trough:** minor trough two lower than minor troughs one and three.
- **peak:** minor peak two higher than minor peaks one and three.
- **relevance to channels**: as many of these intermediate troughs/peaks as possible should touch boundaries of intermediate term channels.

- **major troughs/peaks:** three successive intermediate troughs/peaks in the correct relationship.
- **trough:** intermediate trough two lower than intermediate troughs one and three.
- **peak:** intermediate peak two higher than intermediate peaks one and three.
- **relevance to channels:** as many of these major troughs/peaks as possible should touch boundaries of long term channels.

Naturally, what is meant by short, intermediate and long term channels depends upon the characteristics of the particular share being studied. In the example we are using in this chapter, Racal, we shall be concerned only with intermediate and long term channels when using weekly data for the analysis. The short term channels can only be defined with any degree of accuracy by using daily data, and these are discussed towards the end of this chapter.

Examples at various points in the Racal price history

The way in which channel analysis is used to predict price movements is best illustrated by using the Racal chart as an example, taking several points at various times along the period covered by the chart. Since most readers will not have access to a computer or chart plotting and moving average calculating software, these analyses will be carried out by drawing the channels by eye. The object of the analysis is to draw attention to the imminence of turning points, but of course since turning points occur relatively infrequently, most of the time the decision following from the analysis is that the price is expected to continue in the same direction. The first examples use weekly data, and it should be noted that there will be slightly more error involved in the determination of turning points using weekly data compared with daily data. Nevertheless, these examples serve to show the power of the method even when weekly data is used for the analysis.

September 9th 1983 (price: 234p)

The chart from mid-1982 until September 9th 1983 is shown in Figure 4.3. It is possible to construct two channels for the Racal price over this time period, an inner channel and an outer channel. The inner channel is constructed by drawing the upper boundary so as to touch as many of the peaks as possible, bearing in mind the necessity to draw a smooth curve, and the same approach is used for the lower boundary. The width of the channel as measured vertically, has to be kept constant, and in the present case is about 35p in

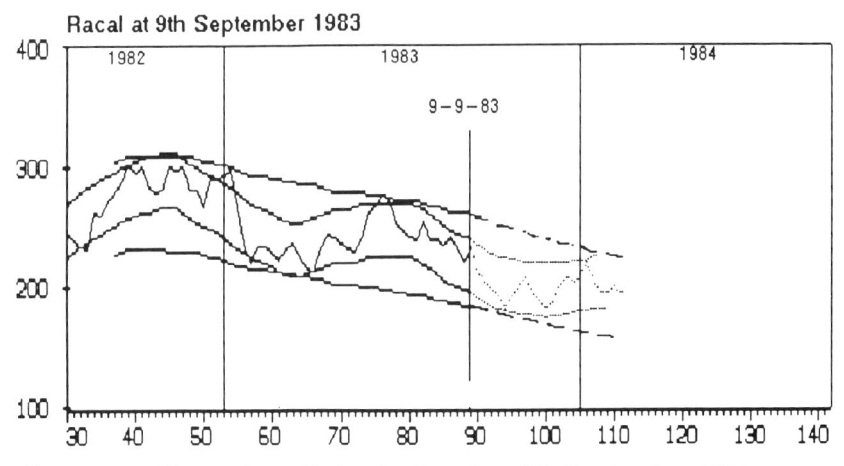

Figure 4.3. Channel prediction for Racal on 9th September 1983.

vertical width. This requirement to maintain a constant vertical width may necessitate redrawing parts of the channel, the over-riding aim being to enclose as much of the price movement as possible. Note that if the inclusion of one or two peaks or troughs of extreme movement would make the channel too wide, these should be allowed to overshoot or undershoot the channel to keep the width tighter.

As we progress along the chart, there will be occasions where the upper boundary will be better defined than the lower boundary, due to the closeness of successive peaks. On other occasions the lower boundary will be easier to draw. Adopt the approach of drawing the easiest boundary for each part of the price history and drawing the other boundary at the constant width above or below it as the case may be, the complete picture being then a much more realistic channel than if you try to draw it all in one go. By this means the inner channel should appear like that in Figure 4.3. Predicted channels are drawn as dotted lines. Actual price movement is also shown as a dotted line. Just as we drew the inner channel by drawing smooth curves to enclose most of the price movement, so we can draw an outer channel by drawing smooth curves to enclose the inner channel itself. This has also been done in Figure 4.3. Prediction of price movements in the immediate future is then done by extrapolating both the outer and inner channels with smooth lines forward in time as shown by the dotted and dashed lines in the Figure. Since the inner channel has two peaks about 35 weeks apart in time, it is reasonable to suppose that the next trough in the inner channel should occur about this same distance in the future from the last trough, and this takes us to a point about seven weeks ahead of the present date. By observing where the outer channel is at this point in time, the touching point of these two channels will give us a fix on the range into which the price will move, and this will be about 160-170p. Our prediction therefore is that about 28th October, give or take a week or so, the share price of Racal should bottom out at about 160-170p.

This particular date was taken as an example because it happened to be just a few weeks prior to a turning point in the intermediate cycles in the Racal price, and this also coincided with a turning point in the longer term cycle. Part of the uncertainty of price prediction lies in the fact that channels can suddenly develop an upward or downward hook which is not predictable. Because of this, our prediction of the turning point in the Racal price is fairly accurate, but the lowest price level reached was higher than than anticipated. This does not matter too much in the present example, since the prime objective was to determine the beginning of a new upward trend. Bearing this in mind, we can now observe, as shown by the dotted line in Figure 4.3 how the price behaved in the weeks following the date on which the prediction was made. The first feature we come to in the following weeks is a trough, at 184p, five weeks later on October 14th 1983. Naturally we do not know it was a trough until six weeks on, i.e. on October 21st, when the price closes higher (194p) than the previous week (184p). Since we are now watching most carefully for the turning point in the price, this trough may be the turning point, although we expected the turn to come four or five weeks later. Obviously, we are not able to define the turning point in the price until after the event, i.e. the turning point is only defined by the fact that the next trough is higher. The next trough, on 25th November at 185p (only defined as a trough once we see that the price on 2nd December is higher) does turn out to be higher, and therefore this fact now defines the previous one, on 14th October as being the turning point in the Racal share price. The actual bottom Friday closing price, on 14th October was 184p, compared with the predicted price of 160-170p. By channel analysis we were certain by 2nd December that the bottom had been reached on 14th October. This is a smaller delay than would have been achieved by means of moving average calculations, and serves to show the power of the technique.

Note that the delay in determining the bottom was totally beyond our control, since it was dependent upon the need for two successive troughs to be formed in order to define the turning point. If these two troughs had been two or three weeks closer together in time, then our delay would have been two or three weeks less.

Once the change in direction of the price has been observed, then naturally the drawn channels can be adjusted from their predicted positions to their actual positions. This then gives us much more valuable data with which to continue the analysis to the next point.

March 30th 1984 (price: 215p)

The chart relevant to a prediction at this point in time is shown in Figure 4.4. As we discussed above, the two troughs on 14th October and 25th November established that the longer term outside channel had changed direction, because these troughs, within the inside channel, had not descended as low as predicted. Our attention will now have turned to keeping a close watch on troughs and peaks in order to continuously re-adjust our projection of the inner channel with a view to predicting the next period at which it will approach the outer channel boundary. The troughs on 10th February at 194p and 23rd March at 207p gives us a good fix on the current direction. The upper boundary has fewer decisive peaks to enable its construction, and therefore the principle of maintaining a constant width remains paramount in determining its position. On this criterion, the peak on 6th January at 222p will project slightly above the "best" channel boundary. This extrapolation of the inner and outer channels leads us to predict that the inner upper will touch the outer upper boundary about eight weeks into the future, about 25th May 1984. The

Racal at 30th March 1984

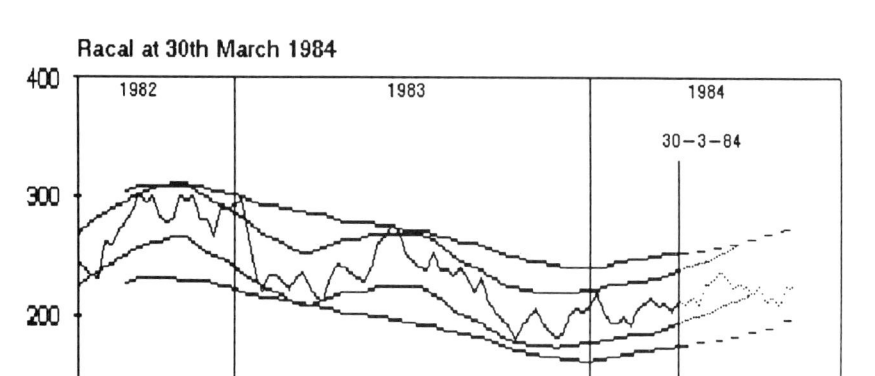

Figure 4.4. Channel prediction for Racal on 30th March 1984.

predicted price range is 240-250p. The actual peak price (on weekly data) was 238p, reached two weeks before the predicted time, on 11th May 1984.

Taking stock of our two predictions so far of the Racal share price, we note two difficulties. Firstly the actual trough or peak occurred a few weeks sooner than predicted, and secondly, the price fell short of these predictions. In the absence of any proper strategy for dealing with such situations, the danger would be that we would shelve our buying or selling decision in the expectation that our predictions are perfect and that a better price will be available by the actual predicted time. However, a useful historical fact about the Racal share price will be of great help: the intermediate price peaks and troughs are reached in a relatively smooth transition, and rarely does the price dip a week or two before the real peak or rise a week or two before the real trough. Therefore in the current two predicted situations, the rise or fall from the trough or peak would be a signal that we have already passed the predicted point, and should therefore take appropriate action. There is one further point to be made, and that is that we are dealing with weekly data, so that we naturally have a greater error in both predicted times and prices compared with using daily data. As discussed later, the most appropriate strategy is to use weekly data to give predictions of peaks and troughs, but to use daily data to carry us forward from the time at which we make the prediction. By doing this we shall be able to achieve slightly better buying and selling performance. However, for the present exercise, we can take this as read, and simply show how we can continue to predict future prices with reasonable accuracy from weekly data.

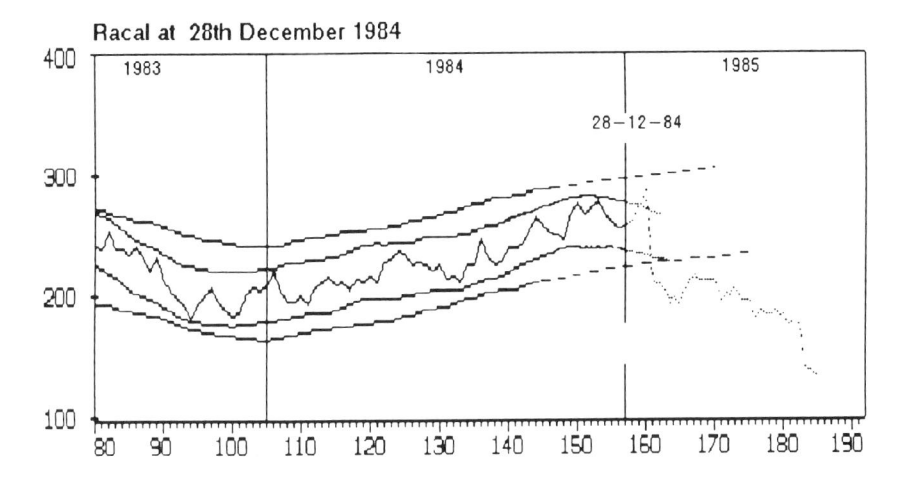

Figure 4.5. Channel prediction for Racal on 28th December 1984.

December 28th 1984 (price:260p)

This point was chosen for the analysis since it was two weeks prior to a particularly steep fall in the Racal share price at the beginning of 1985. The fall was so steep that the first reaction is that no method of price prediction could deal with it. However, as we will see, investors following the method of channel analysis would have come out of the share the very first day that the price fell back from the peak. For the twenty or thirty weeks prior to the prediction date, the inner channel is particularly well defined, since we have three troughs and three peaks that almost exactly coincide with the channel boundaries using the principle of constant channel width.

The troughs are: 13th July (212p), 17th August (226p), 26th October (248p) and 21st December (256p). The peaks are : 11th June (238p), 3rd August (248p), 28th September (266p), 9th November (278p) and 30th November (280p). The peak on 30th November is vital, since the curve which was already apparent from drawing the smoothest line through the previous three peaks is now forced into a sharper radius by the failure of this peak to rise above 280p. The inner channel can therefore be extrapolated with reasonable accuracy into the near future, the important aspect being that it has reached a maximum for the time being. This being the case, all we are waiting for in our predicted price movement is a close approach to the upper boundary. A predicted date can be put on this point by reference to the distance between the last two troughs, which is eight weeks. It is reasonable to expect that the next peak will be this distance forward in time from the last peak, i.e. eight weeks forward from 30th November 1984, which takes us to 25th January 1985. Our prediction is therefore one week too late, since the peak, as far as weekly data is concerned occurred on 18th January 1985. In practice, we have said that in order to retain maximum sensitivity, we would be operating on daily data once we have drawn the projected channels, and therefore we would be preparing to exit from Racal the instant the price fell back from the upper channel boundary. The more conservative investor might well adopt a policy of selling as soon as a boundary is reached.

August 23rd 1985 (price:160p)

This is at a rather interesting part of the overall chart of Racal, because it will have taken over five months before the lower boundary of the inner channel was really defined. Since, as we have stated before, it takes at least two troughs or peaks to define a boundary, then following the trough on the 8th February at 192p, it was not until 24th July that the next trough was formed at 132p so that a clearly defined channel could be drawn. Obviously at the time of prediction on 23rd August we are at a point near the upper boundary of the inner channel. In the very short term therefore we can expect the price to fall to the lower boundary, which at the predicted rate of curvature will fall to about 125-130p before rising again, as can be seen by the extrapolated channel in the Figure. As can be seen from the Figure, the price does fall to a minimum of

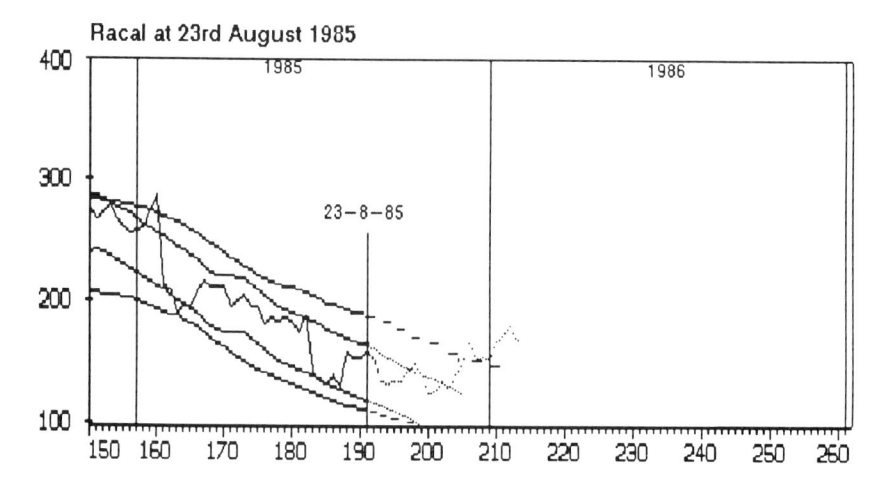

Figure 4.6. Channel prediction for Racal on 23rd August 1985.

128p nine weeks later on 25th October. The longer term implication for the share price can be seen from the fact that this turning point represents the bottom of the outside channel. This means that the price can be expected to carry on rising past 200p. That this happens can be seen from the subsequent price movement shown in Figure 4.6.

April 18th 1986 (price: 206p)

Crucial to the prediction of prices from this point onwards is the previous trough on 28th March 1986 at 180p. This defines the lower boundary of the inner channel quite clearly. In the short term the expectation is for a price reversal as soon as the upper boundary is reached. This happened two weeks hence from the prediction date, on 2nd May when the price reached was 224p.

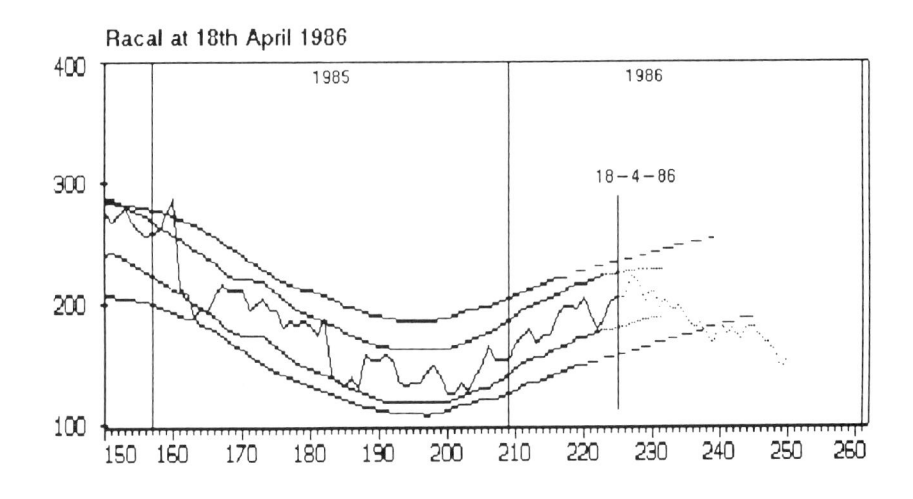

Figure 4.7. Channel prediction for Racal on 18th April 1986.

September 19th 1986 (price: 172p)

Since the previous peak on 2nd May 1986, the only significant trough occurred on 25th July 1986, at 170p. Since this was much lower than that predicted by the extrapolated channel in the previous prediction on 18th April, we now have to adjust the inner channel by causing it to curve downwards so as to incorporate this low reading in the lower boundary. Previous important trough-to-trough distances over the past year or so were about 9 weeks and 17 weeks, these occurring several times. Although we cannot be sure which of

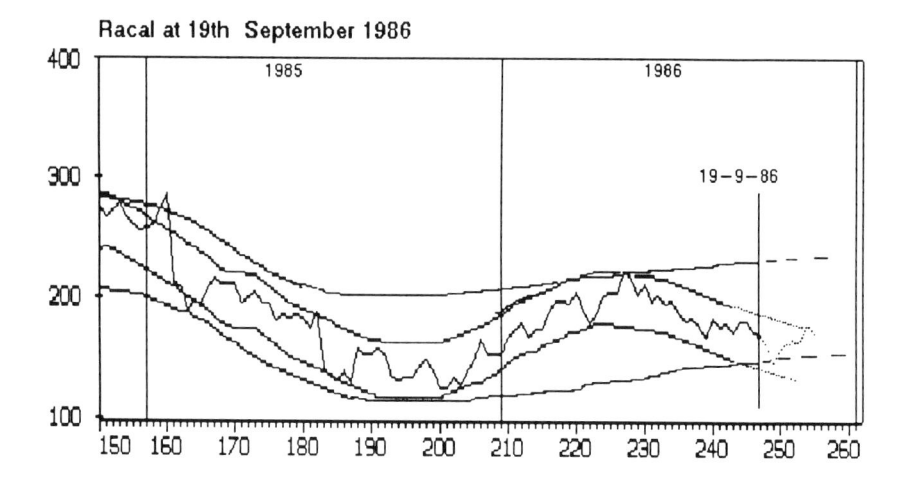

Figure 4.8. Channel prediction for Racal on 19th September 1986.

these might be the more dominant at the present time, we must err on the side of caution and at least be prepared for the next trough to occur nine weeks on from the last one, i.e. on 26th September, and at a price somewhere around 145 to 150p. As can be seen from the Figure, the trough did not occur until a week later, but we were spot on in the price since it reached a low of 148p. Note that at the predicted time, 26th September, the price at 162p was so far above the predicted boundary that it would have been quite reasonable to have waited until the situation was resolved. The fact that this low point of 148p was higher than the previous major low point a year previously (128p on 25th October 1985) shows that the outer channel, which of necessity must pass through the major troughs and peaks, is now started on an uptrend. This low point is therefore a prime investment buying point.

September/October 1987

This point, taken as being just prior to the October Crash, will be dealt with shortly as a prime example of the advantage of using daily data rather than weekly data for predicting price movements. The rate of fall of prices during the crash was such that no analysis based upon weekly data could hope to anticipate.

January 1st 1988

The uptrend established in the outer channel following the low point of 3rd October 1986 requires a more recent trough in order to define it with greater

Racal at 1st January 1988

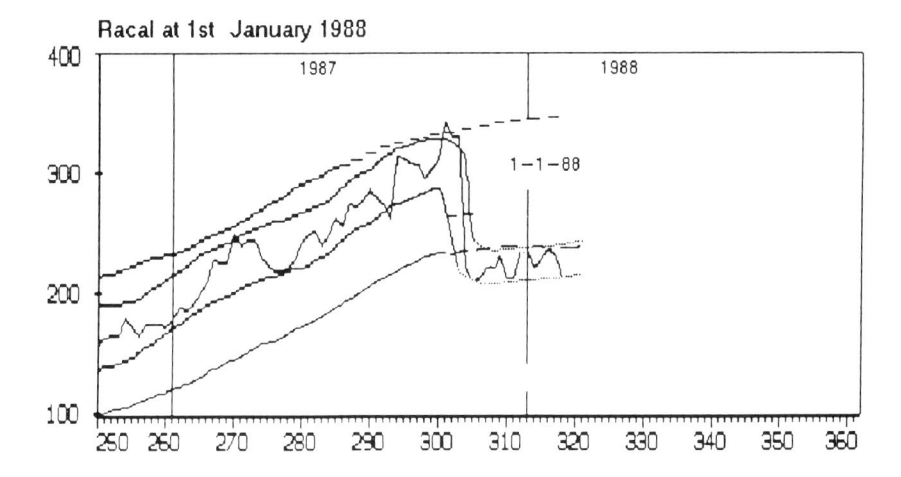

Figure 4.9. Channel prediction for Racal on 1st January 1988.

accuracy. Quite obviously the low point on 4th December 1987 does just this. We can now see that in spite of the rapid fall due to the crash, the outer channel is still headed firmly upwards, and that, since the low in December is obviously a low point in the inner channel, then the price can be expected to move upwards over the following few weeks. Projection of the outer channel gives an upper level to the share price of around 300p, and we might expect this to occur about six months into the future, based on the fact that the distance between the last two troughs is about one year, so the trough-to-peak distance should be half of this.

Improved Accuracy Using Daily Data

We have already mentioned briefly that powerful though the technique of channel analysis is, there are still uncertainties in the prediction of stock market prices. The uncertainty lies in both the timing and the extent of a price trend. A channel can develop an extreme downward or upward hook which was not predictable. However, if the hook is preceeded by indications that the price has reached a channel boundary, then this should mean that the investor, although unaware of the impending dramatic over-reaction, will have already taken action. Channel analysis will then have protected the investor against such drastic overshoots.

In the case of a trough or peak being several weeks too early or too late compared with the predicted time, the usual cause is the (unpredictable) increasing importance of short term cycles. Since short term cycles are most accurately described when daily data is used, then quite obviously, it is

54 TRADED OPTIONS SIMPLIFIED

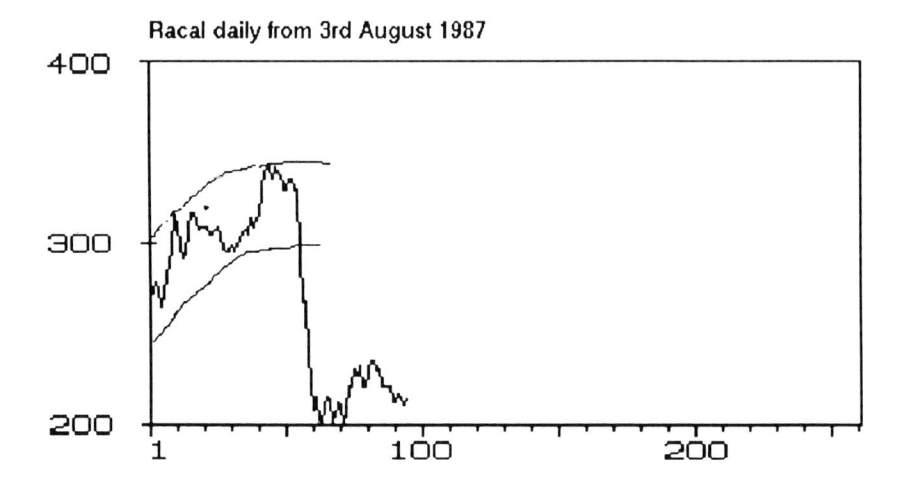

Figure 4.10. The clearer impression of short term movements in the Racal share price when daily data is used.

imperative to use daily data when a predicted trough or peak is only a few weeks away in time.

Quite obviously the most stringent test that could be applied to channel analysis is the situation just prior to the crash of October 1987. In Figure 4.10 are shown the channels drawn on a chart where daily data has been plotted from August 1987. The two important points we would like to clarify are firstly, whether we would have been given any indication that the crash was imminent, and secondly how quickly after the crash we could have come to a firm decision about the future course of the Racal share price. Although daily data is being used, this will not affect the width of the channels which we have been studying until now using weekly data. We still see this same channel in Figure 4.10, but note that we can see much more detail of price movements within the channel. Just prior to the October crash, we can see at the left hand side of the chart that there was a wave within the channel, which had its two successive troughs about fifteen days apart. Because of the fine detail, we can also see much more clearly that the next wave had reached its peak about five or six days before the Black Monday crash. Of course, what we would not have known at the time, because there was no evidence to show this, was that the channel itself was about to do anything but continue in its gentle curve that we would have expected to top out some twenty or thirty weeks into the future. Thus the conclusion we would have drawn from the data would be that, five or six days before the crash, we were reaching the top of a channel that itself was beginning to look a bit toppy, but had some more upward potential in it. At this point, the most likely situation would be that investors simply holding Racal shares would continue to do so in the expectation of squeezing a little more extra profit before it became time to sell. It would have been investors in traded options who would have been the most likely to have taken action. Note that the cycles of fifteen days that we mentioned had a trough to peak difference of about 50p, i.e. about 15% or so of the price, and this is a very significant movement in an underlying share price as far as traded options are concerned. Thus holders of call options should have been considering selling these as the upper boundary of the projected channel was approached, while others would have been interested in buying put options at this level, since the expectation was for a fall of 40-50p down the second half of the 15 day cycle. The conclusion therefore is that Racal shareholders might not have avoided the crash even with channel analysis using daily data, but that traded options investors would have done so.

As far as the post-crash position was concerned, it is interesting to see at what point a prediction as to future price movements could have been made. First of all we had to wait for the price to stop its free-fall action and make a rise, however small, thus defining a minor trough in the price. This minor trough can then be considered to be on the lower boundary of the channel, thus helping to define it. At this point in time we have two vital observations that will help in predicting the future movement. Firstly, the inner channel has obviously just peaked out, and is now headed downwards. Secondly, we can turn our attention to the longer term outer channel. We now have three peaks and two troughs in the inner channel which will define this outer channel with a rough degree of accuracy. We can see that because the latest peak in October is higher than the previous peak, the outer channel must still be headed upwards in spite of the crash. Naturally, there is still some chance that this channel may develop a sudden hook just like the inner channel, but this is something we cannot predict and therefore have to ignore at this point in time. This upwards headed lower boundary therefore gives us a floor for the behaviour of the inner channel, and therefore some indication as to the behaviour of the share price itself. At this point, we are still lacking any degree of accuracy, since we have only one minor trough following the crash, and this is not sufficient to define the degree of curvature that we have to adopt for the inner channel. Once we have a second trough, we can then draw the inner channel much more realistically and also predict the point at which it should reach the lower boundary of the outer channel and start to curve back upwards.

At this point in time, where we are awaiting a second trough to be formed that will define the inner channel, we can take advantage of having daily data for the analysis and construct another channel inside what we have been calling the inner channel. This could not be done with weekly data because the periodicity of some of the movements is measured in days rather than weeks.

We already briefly mentioned this narrower channel in discussing the 15 day cycle prior to the crash. This cycle had a trough to peak difference of about 50p, but the channel containing this cycle will be narrower because of the upward direction at the pre-crash point. The width of this third channel is about 30p, and at the latest point at which daily data was available, the 30th January 1988, the channel is shown in Figure 4.10. It can be seen quite clearly that at that date, this channel has already passed its peak and is on the way down. We can therefore project it into the near future with reasonable accuracy, and since the time from trough to peak is about five weeks and we are about two weeks past this peak, we predict is will turn up again about three weeks on from 30th January. This future low point then gives us an indication of the time and extent of the next trough that we are awaiting before we can define the inner channel with greater accuracy. We can now, as shown in Figure 4.10, project this inner channel into the future.

The net effect of these predictions of a very short term channel, our more usual inner channel and the long term outer channel is that we expect the Racal share price to drift slowly downwards for the next thirty weeks or so and then begin a decisive move upwards to at least 250p. The target date for this is therefore about the end of August 1988.

This example of Racal serves to show quite clearly what can be achieved by using channel analysis compared with simple moving averages, and also the advantage that can be obtained by using daily data for the plots when approaching key predicted turning points. You should also begin to see that as we progress along the price history of a share, we will have greater or lesser degrees of certainty not so much about the direction of a trend, but about the target price for the trend. We should try to quantify this degree of certainty, because, as shown in the next chapter, it is crucial to understanding the amount of risk that we should take on board in our traded option strategy.

CHAPTER 5

Relationship Between Share and Option Prices

Once an investor has come to a conclusion about the probable future course of a share price, and decides he wishes to take advantage of the opportunities offered by investing in traded options, he is faced with a bewildering array of options from which to choose. There are call options and put options, various striking prices and various expiry dates, and the major difficulty is in deciding which of these is appropriate. However, behind the apparent chaos, there is a great deal of logic to the way in which options are priced. A careful consideration of the relationship between option prices and the underlying share prices will lead to a much better view of which is the correct option for a particular set of investment circumstances.

INTRINSIC VALUES AND TIME VALUES

The investor who has selected the share and taken a decision about the future movement of that share price has at this point simply reached an opinion. From now on his decision as to the exact option he will buy will depend upon facts. These are only four in number:

1. The share price.
2. The option striking prices.
3. The option expiry dates.
4. The premiums for the various option series.

The inter-relationship between these four facts is extremely subtle, but to ensure maximum profit at the degree of risk which the investor is prepared to accept requires a detailed attention to this relationship. As in any other stock market, there is no cut and dried formula which always works; it is possible however to arrive at a highly probably outcome. Those three items which have a numerical value, viz. the share price, striking price and premium can be used in a simple sense to calculate two further quantities, the intrinsic value and the time value for a particular series. For a call option, the intrinsic value increases as the share price rises, while for a put option the intrinsic value increases as the share price falls. In addition to the intrinsic value, options have a time value

58 TRADED OPTIONS SIMPLIFIED

Table 5.1. Intrinsic values for some call options on 5th February 1988.

Share	Share Price	Strike Price	Intrinsic Value
Allied Lyons	332	300	32
		330	2
		360	0
Brit. Aerospace	356	330	26
		360	0
		390	0
Amstrad	144	130	14
		140	4
		160	0

which decreases the closer the expiry date approaches, irrespective of whether they are call or put options.

Intrinsic Value of Call options

Since a call option gives the holder the right to buy shares of the underlying security at a predetermined fixed price, then naturally this call option becomes more valuable as the share price rises. The intrinsic value of a call option is simply given by the relationship:

Intrinsic value = share price - strike price

Where the strike price is equal to or greater than the share price, then obviously the intrinsic value is zero. Negative values of course have no meaning other than zero. It is only when the share price is greater than the strike price that there is an intrinsic value. Thus, taking as an example the three Bass April calls of 750, 800 and 850, we find on February 5th 1988 the share price was 780p. By the above definition, we see that the 750 call has an intrinsic value of 30p while the others have no intrinsic value. This is of course perfectly logical, since on February 5th we could exercise the option to buy Bass shares at 750p when their market value is 30p higher at 780p. Obviously we would not exercise the 800 and 850 options since if we required Bass shares, we could buy them cheaper at the market price of 780p. Just to make sure that intrinsic values are clearly understood, in Table 5.1 are shown a number of examples of share prices, strike prices and intrinsic values. Remembering our definition of in-the-money, out-of-the-money and at-the-money call options given in Chapter 2, we can see that the intrinsic value of at-the-money options (strike

```
INTRINSIC
VALUE
  100 ─

   75 ─

   50 ─

   25 ─

    0 ─┼────────┼────────┼────────┼────────┼
       200      250      300      350
                        SHARE PRICE
```

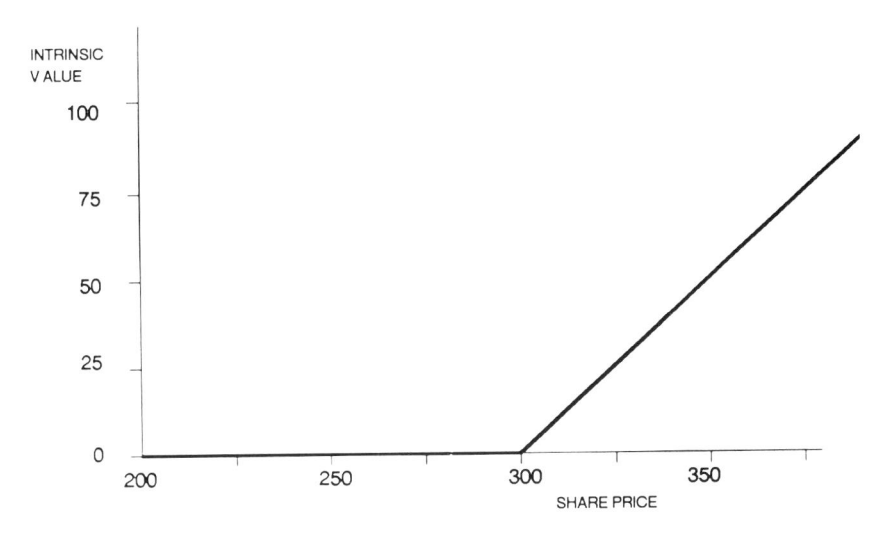

Figure 5.1. Intrinsic value of Allied Lyons April 300 call option with changing share price.

price equal to the share price) and out-of-the-money options (strike price higher than the share price) is zero in each case. Only in-the-money call options (strike price below the share price) have an intrinsic value. The concept of intrinsic value can be depicted graphically as shown in Figure 5.1. Here we have taken the Allied Lyons April 300 Call option (although the expiry date does not matter for this exercise) and show the effect of an increase in the share price on the intrinsic value. The intrinsic value stays at zero until the share price reaches 300p. The line then rises at a slope of 45 degrees, since every 10p excess of share price over 300p gives an increase in intrinsic value of 10p.

Time value of Call Options

If an out-of-the-money option has no intrinsic value, one may well ask why it still commands a premium. The answer lies in the expectation that in the course of time, or rather in the course of the time remaining to the expiry date, the share price will rise above the strike price, thereby turning the option into an in-the-money option which therefore will have an intrinsic value. Thus the amount of time remaining to the expiry date has a value, which differs from one option to another, and which is called the time value. The time value can be defined as:

Time value = option premium - intrinsic value

Table 5.2. Intrinsic values and time values for a number of call options on 5th February 1988.

Share (price)	Striking price	Expiry date	Premium	Intrinsic value	Time value
Allied Lyons (332p)	300	April	45	32	13
		July	48	32	16
		October	58	32	26
	330	April	23	2	21
		July	30	2	28
		October	40	2	38
	360	April	11	0	11
		July	18	0	18
		October	28	0	28
Brit Aero (356p)	330	February	28	26	2
		May	44	26	18
		August	55	26	29
	360	February	9	0	9
		May	27	0	27
		August	40	0	40
	390	February	2	0	2
		May	13	0	13
		August	28	0	28
Amstrad (144p)	130	March	19	14	5
		June	25	14	11
		September	31	14	17
	140	March	12	4	8
		June	19	4	15
		September	26	4	22
	160	March	5	0	5
		June	12	0	12
		September	19	0	19

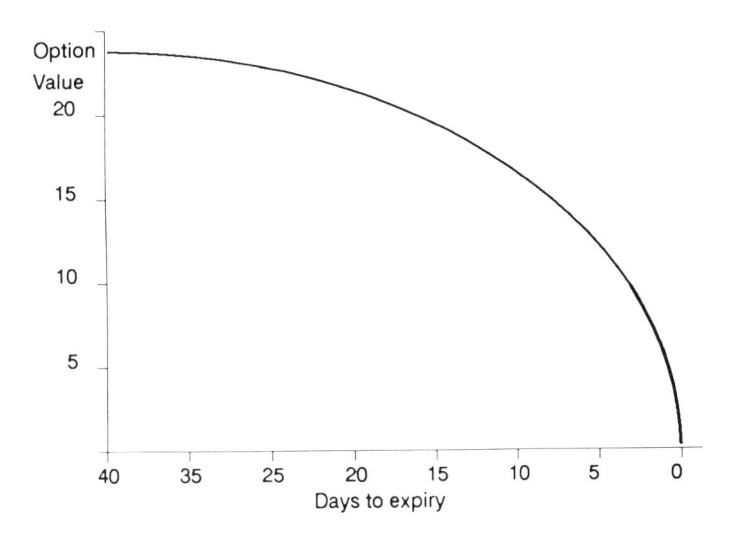

```
Option
Value
 20

 15

 10

  5

     40   35   25   20   15   10    5    0
                  Days to expiry
```

Figure 5.2. The falling value of Allied Lyons call options as expiry day approaches. Share price is assumed to be a constant 330p.

For at-the-money and out-of-the-money options, where as we said above the intrinsic values are zero, the relationship becomes:

Time value = option premium

From the relationship between premium, intrinsic value and time value, it can be seen that a higher intrinsic value (more in-the-money) will naturally lead to a higher premium. It should also be seen that the higher the time value, the higher the premium. The time value is a reflection of the amount of time remaining until an option expires. Therefore a November option in a particular share will have a higher time value than the equivalent August option. Similarly a May option will have a greater time value than an equivalent February option. This reflects the fact that where a considerable time is left to the expiry date, there is more chance that a price movement in the underlying share will occur in the anticipated direction. Quite obviously, the most expensive premiums are for the deepest in-the-money options with the longest time to expiry. Conversely, the cheapest options are those which are furthest out-of-the-money and with the shortest time to expiry. In Table 5.2 are shown the premiums, intrinsic values and the calculated time values for the Allied Lyons, British Aerospace and Amstrad call options. While certain general conclusions can be drawn, and these are in line with expectation, a more specific relationship between time values and share price cannot be deduced. In the case of British Aerospace, the extra six months given by the August over the February option is worth an increase in time value of 27p, 31p and 26p for the 330, 360 and 390 calls respectively relative to a share price of 356p. This gives an average for the time value of 28p, and relative to the share price gives a value of 7.86%. In the case of Amstrad, the extra six months given by the September over the March option is worth an increase in time value of 12p, 14p and 14p for the 130, 140 and 160 calls respectively relative to a share price of 144p. This gives an average for the time value of 13.33p, and relative to the share price gives a value of 9.26%. In the case of Allied Lyons options, the extra six months given by the October option over the April option is worth an increase in time value of 15p, 17p and 17p for the 300, 330 and 360 calls respectively relative to a share price of 332p. This gives an average for the time value of 16.33p, and relative to the share price gives a value of 4.9%. It is possible to explain the difference between British Aerospace and Amstrad on the basis of the first having its furthest out option with an August expiry date, and the second a September expiry date. We would then expect the Allied Lyons case, with October being the furthest out expiry date to put a larger value percentage-wise on the time value, whereas it is the smallest. On this basis therefore the Allied Lyons case is out of line.

Time values can be depicted graphically as shown in Figure 5.2, where we take the Allied Lyons April 330 call options. For this exercise, we have to assume a constant share price of 330p in order to show the variation of the option price with time. As expiry day approaches, the option value, which consists of time value plus intrinsic value, falls due to the fall in time value, until on expiry day, its value is just the intrinsic value.

For out-of-the-money options, the time value remains approximately constant until about six or eight weeks before expiry, when it then starts to fall rapidly, becoming, of course, zero at expiry date. The premiums for nine month, six month and three month options for out-of-the-money options (i.e. those with no intrinsic value and whose premiums are solely due to time value) can be in a ratio as high as 3 to 2 to 1, while options which are more or less at-the-money will have a ratio round about 2 to 1.5 to 1 and in-the-money options closer than this in value. Although only a rough guide, this is very useful in helping to decide whether a particular premium is out of line with expectation. There is one further aspect that we have yet to consider in this discussion of premiums, and that is the nature of the underlying share. If we take two shares which are standing at the same price and have similar option series, then we would be unlikely to find that each series has the same premium. In general, the more volatile the share, the higher will be the premium for a particular option series. However, since the intrinsic value for the option series of the respective shares are calculated only from the share price and the strike price, which are identical, then the intrinsic values will be the same. Because

Table 5.3. Intrinsic values for a number of put options on 5th February 1988.

Share	Share Price	Strike Price	Intrinsic Value
Allied Lyons	332	300	0
		330	0
		360	28
Brit. Aerospace	356	330	0
		360	4
		390	34
Amstrad	144	130	0

of this fact, the effect of the differing volatility of the shares is to be found incorporated into the time values.

premium 1 = intrinsic value 1 + time value 1

premium 2 = intrinsic value 2 + time value 2

if premium 1 is not equal to premium 2, then time value 1 is not equal to time value 2

Since the timescales are identical, then time value 1 includes some value for volatility of share 1 and time value 2 includes some value for volatility of share 2. It is important therefore that some measure of volatility is kept for each security listed (42 at the time of writing) on the London Traded Options list. The simplest way of doing this is to calculate the ratio of the high to low value of each security for the current year. If values of this ratio for several years is available, then average out these ratios over say four or five years. The securities can then be listed in decreasing magnitude of this ratio, i.e. the most volatile at the top of the list. Frequently situations can be found in which the premium is an incorrect reflection of the volatility of the share, and such situations can usually be turned to advantage.

Put Options

The above discussions of intrinsic values and time values apply only to call options. The relationship between share prices, strike prices, premiums,

64 TRADED OPTIONS SIMPLIFIED

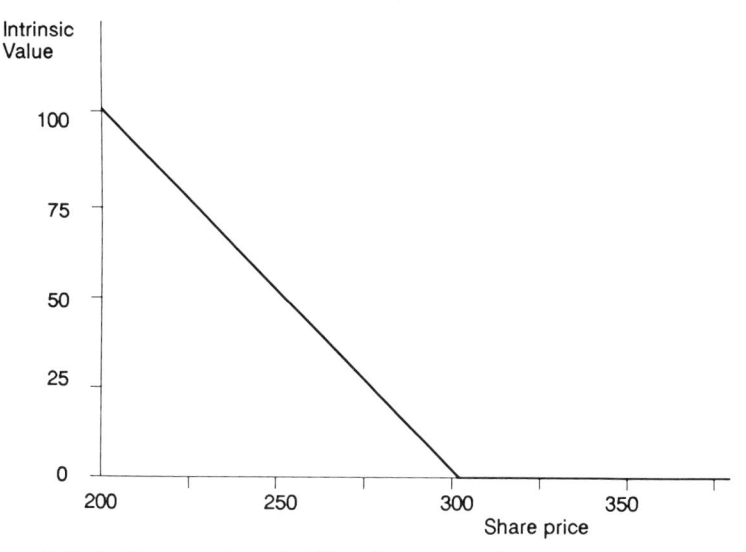

Figure 5.3. Intrinsic value of Allied Lyons April 330 put option with changing share price.

intrinsic values and time values is different for put options. A put option becomes more valuable as the share price falls.

The intrinsic value of a put option is therefore given by the relationship:

Intrinsic value = strike price - share price

The intrinsic value is zero for the situation where the strike price is equal to the share price (at-the-money) or where the share price is higher than the strike price (out-of-the-money). It is only where the share price has fallen below the strike price that the option has an intrinsic value. Taking as an example the three Bass April put options of 750, 800 and 850, we find on February 5th 1988 the share price was 780p. On the above definition, we see that the 750 puts had an intrinsic value of zero, the 800 puts an intrinsic value of 20p and the 850 puts an intrinsic value of 70p. In order to help in understanding intrinsic values as applied to put options, in Table 5.3 are shown the intrinsic values of Allied Lyons, British Aerospace and Amstrad puts.

The concept of intrinsic value as applied to put options can be shown graphically as in Figure 5.3. Here we have taken the Allied Lyons April 330 puts and show the effect of an fall in the share price on the intrinsic value. The expiry date has no relevance for this exercise. The intrinsic value stays at zero until the share price falls below 330p. The line then rises at a slope of 45 degrees. This is because every 10p fall in share price leads to a 10p increase in intrinsic value.

SHARE AND OPTION PRICES 65

Table 5.4. Time values for put options on 5th February 1988.

Share (price)	Striking price	Expiry date	Premium	Intrinsic value	Time value
Allied Lyons (332p)	300	April	6	0	6
		July	15	0	15
		October	21	0	21
	330	April	14	2	12
		July	28	2	26
		October	33	2	31
	360	April	35	28	7
		July	45	28	17
		October	50	28	22
Brit Aero (356p)	330	February	1.5	0	1.5
		May	20	0	20
		August	28	0	28
	360	February	14	4	10
		May	37	4	33
		August	45	4	41
	390	February	40	34	6
		May	55	34	21
		August	67	34	33
Amstrad (144p)	130	March	5.5	0	5.5
		June	10	0	10
		September	16	0	16
	140	March	9	0	9
		June	14	0	14
		September	22	0	22
	160	March	21	16	5
		June	25	16	9
		September	37	16	21

66 TRADED OPTIONS SIMPLIFIED

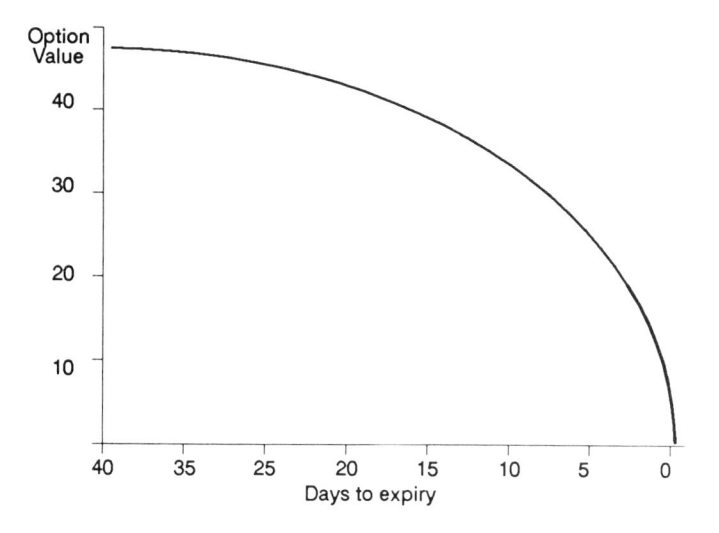

Figure 5.4. The falling value of Allied Lyons 360 put options as expiry date approaches. Share price is assumed to be a constant 330p.

Time Value of Put Options

As with call options, we can use the same argument to explain why there should still be a premium payable for a put option even though it has no intrinsic value. Once again, it is the expectation for the price that generates a premium value. Some investors feel that the price will fall sometime before the expiry of the option, and they are willing to pay money in the form of the premium for the option to back their view of the course of events. Again, as with call options, this remaining time until expiry has a value, which differs from one option to another; this is called the time value.

The time value of a put option can be defined as:

Time value = option premium - intrinsic value

For at-the-money options and out-of-the-money options, where the intrinsic value is zero, the relationship becomes:

Time value = option premium

Just as was the case with call options, it can be seen that a higher intrinsic value (more in-the-money) will lead to a higher premium. Also the higher the time value, the higher the premium. Thus the most expensive options are the deepest in-the-money with the longest time to expiry, while the cheapest are the furthest out-of-the-money which are just about to expire. In Table 5.4 are shown the premiums, intrinsic values and the calculated time values for the Allied Lyons, British Aerospace and Amstrad options. As was the case with call options, while certain general conclusions can be drawn, and these are in line with expectation, a more specific relationship between time values and share price cannot be deduced. In the case of British Aerospace, the extra six months given by the August over the February option is worth an increase in time value of 26.5p, 31p and 27p for the 330, 360 and 390 puts respectively relative to a share price of 356p. This gives an average for the time value of 28p, and relative to the share price gives a value of 7.86%. In the case of Amstrad, the extra six months given by the September over the March option is worth an increase in time value of 10.5p, 13p and 16p for the 130, 140 and 160 puts respectively relative to a share price of 144p. This gives an average for the time value of 13.16p, and relative to the share price gives a value of 9.13%. In the case of Allied Lyons options, the extra six months given by the October option over the April option is worth an increase in time value of 15p, 19p and 15p for the 300, 330 and 360 puts respectively relative to a share price of 332p. This gives an average for the time value of 16.33p, and relative to the share price gives a value of 4.9%. If you refer back to the average time values calculated for the equivalent call options, you will find that they are virtually identical to those calculated for the put options.

The time values of put options can be shown graphically as in Figure 5.4, where we take the Allied Lyons 330 put options. For the purpose of this exercise we have assumed a constant share price of 330p in order to show the variation of the option price with time. As expiry date approaches, the value, which consists of time value plus intrinsic value, falls due to the diminishing time value, until on expiry day, its value is just the intrinsic value.

The same relationship for the nine month, six month and three month option premiums holds as for call options, i.e. they fall in the approximate relationship of 3 to 2 to 1 for out-of-the-money and 2 to 1.5 to 1 for at-the-money options. As was the case with call options, there is a further aspect that we have yet to consider in this discussion of premiums, and that is the nature of the underlying share. If we take two shares which are standing at the same price and have similar put option series, then we would be unlikely to find that each series has the same premium. In general, just as for call options, the more volatile the share, the higher will be the premium for a particular option series. However, since the intrinsic values for the option series of the respective shares are calculated only from the share price and the strike price, which are identical,

68 TRADED OPTIONS SIMPLIFIED

then the intrinsic values will be the same. Because of this fact, the effect of the differing volatility of the shares is to be found incorporated into the time values:

premium 1 = intrinsic value 1 + time value 1

premium 2 = intrinsic value 2 + time value 2

If premium 1 is not equal to premium 2, then time value 1 is not equal to time value 2.

Since the timescales are identical, then time value 1 includes some value for volatility of share 1 and time value 2 includes some value for volatility of share 2.

As was stressed for call options, the measure of volatility for each share based upon the ratio of the high to low value of each security for the current year is very useful. Frequently situations can be found in which the premium is an incorrect reflection of the volatility of the share, and such situations can usually be turned to advantage.

CORRELATION BETWEEN OPTION AND SHARE PRICES.

It would be perfectly logical to assume that there is a simple direct relationship between share prices and call option prices and a simple inverse relationship between share prices and put option prices. We would therefore expect that if the share price rises by a small amount, then so should the price of a call option, while the price of a put option should fall. Conversely, if the share price falls, then the price of a call option should fall and the price of a put option should rise. Naturally, the effect of gearing should magnify the responses of the options if these responses are expressed as percentage changes, but we would still, on a simple view, expect that a penny change in share price should cause a penny change in the option price, either upwards or downwards. Some further thought on this subject should lead us to a further conclusion that of course, the options themselves are subject to their own individual supply and demand, which might from time to time, depending upon the circumstances, be independent of the supply and demand position of the underlying shares. In such a situation, the option price might move independently of the share price to a limited extent. Certain investors have a knack of spotting when an option price is out of line with the price or direction of movement of the underlying shares. Working on the assumption that all things eventually find their own level, and that the anomaly will disappear, they can fairly consistently make a profitable investment in such options. As is apparent from the preceeding chapters of this book, our approach is quite different. We have illustrated methods of determining when share price movements will change direction, and the approximate length of time for which the new direction will continue, as well as the new target area for the share price. Quite clearly therefore, we are concerned with options which behave themselves, moving consistently in the same direction (for call options) or the opposite direction (for put options) as the share price, and also moving, as far as possible, penny for penny with the share price. Options which do not do this have to be avoided in favour of those that do. We therefore have to find some method of deciding which options will behave logically. The answer lies in the statistical technique of correlation. There are quite complex statistical methods which can be employed which are tedious unless carried out on a computer, but for our purposes a simple, graphical approach which does not require 'A' level mathematics is perfectly adequate. The Greek letter delta is widely used in science and mathematics to mean the amount of change in a quantity. As far as options are concerned, delta means the change that will occur in the option price for a small change in the share price, assuming other factors to be constant. Theoretical deltas for call options range from 0 to 1, while for put options values range from 0 to -1. The negative value of the latter reflects the fact that the put options lose value as the share price increases, while of course call options gain value with rising share price, and therefore have positive deltas. A delta value of 1 means that a call option gains 1p in value for every 1p rise in the share price, while a delta value of 0 means that the call option price remains unchanged for a 1p rise in the share price. Note here the reason why we use a small change in the share price in order to determine delta values - a large change, say 50p for example, will have an effect on all options, however far out-of-the-money they may be, and so would render meaningless a delta calculated on such a basis. A deep in-the-money call option, with high intrinsic value, should have a delta value of 1, since every 1p rise in share price will give a 1p rise in the option price. There is obviously a strong relationship between option price and share price. On the other hand, a far out-of-the-money option with no intrinsic value, will show a zero rise for a 1p rise in share price, i.e. a delta of 0. There is then a very weak relationship between option and share prices. Obviously, options between these two extremes will have delta values other than 0 or 1. For example at-the-money options should have a delta of 0.5. These delta values can be computed approximately from perusal of daily option prices in the quality newspapers by looking for small changes (1 to 3p) in the share prices and relating all changes to a notional change of 1p in the share price (i.e. for a 3p share price change, divide the option price change by 3). For put options, the delta values are based on the rise in option price for a fall in share price, and have negative values. Thus a heavily in-the-money put option with a high intrinsic value will have a delta of -1, while a heavily out-of-the-money option has a delta of 0. At-the-money options have deltas of -0.5. The above theoretical discussion is useful for giving an insight into the relationship between option prices and

70 TRADED OPTIONS SIMPLIFIED

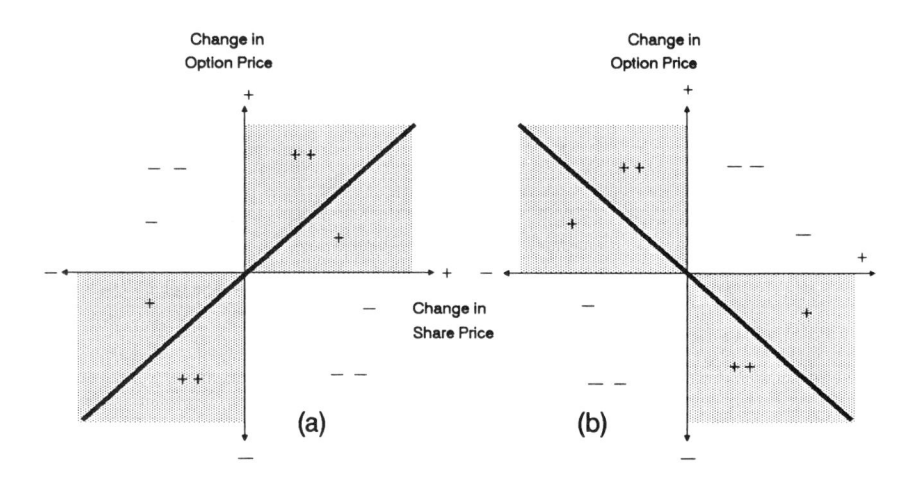

Figure 5.5. Theoretical correlation plots for (a) call options (b) put options. Shaded quadrants have positive correlation and points falling on

share prices, but cannot be carried too far in practical application. As we discussed in the opening section of this chapter, many anomalous situations exist, and it is easy to find in the option price tables in your newspaper call options which rise more than 1p for a 1p rise in the underlying share price, and put options which rise more than 1p for a 1p fall in share price. There are some periods when most options seem to misbehave rather than follow the theoretical relationship discussed above. As we mentioned earlier, this must be due to the unquantifiable effect of supply and demand, a larger than normal demand for an option causing a larger than normal increase in the option price. A more practical method of showing how strong a relationship exists between the option price and the share price is to plot the option price change from one day to the next against the share price change over the corresponding period for both call and put options. Strong and weak correlations can then be easily determined. As stated above, it is essential to stay with those options that exhibit strong correlation ,and avoid those where the correlation is weak. This has the useful effect of reducing the vast array of options available to a much more manageable level, simplifying the task of selecting the correct option for the particular circumstances. Note though that shares which have shown weak correlation in the immediate past can gradually change to a stronger correlation. This means that your current list of 'good' shares should be checked at frequent intervals to weed out any that **are changing their** behaviour. Such shares can then be replaced with some from the 'bad' list that are changing for the better. Two diagrams can be drawn, one for call options and one for put options (Figure 5.5(a) and (b)). The values which are plotted can fall into each of the quadrants shown in the diagrams. The shaded areas represent values which have a positive correlation, while the unshaded areas represent values where there is a negative correlation, for both call and put options. The dashed line at an angle of 45 degrees in each diagram is the line where a change in share price gives exactly the same change in the option price, i.e. delta values of 1 or -1 in terms of the theoretical correlations discussed earlier. When we carry out our plotting of real life share and option prices, we are looking for shares where the majority of the points fall into the shaded areas, since we are looking for positive correlation. If we really wish to fine-tune our selections, we can divide the graph into octants, rather than quadrant. This will highlight shares which show stronger than theoretical correlation (areas marked + +), less than theoretical correlation (areas marked +) and shares which show weak correlation (areas marked -) and very weak correlation (areas marked --). In fact, it might be better to describe shares which fall into the - and -- areas as truly perverse, showing an inverse correlation between option and share prices. For those investors interested in options which are way out of line with expectation, shares which fall into these - and -- sectors offer a fruitful area of investigation.

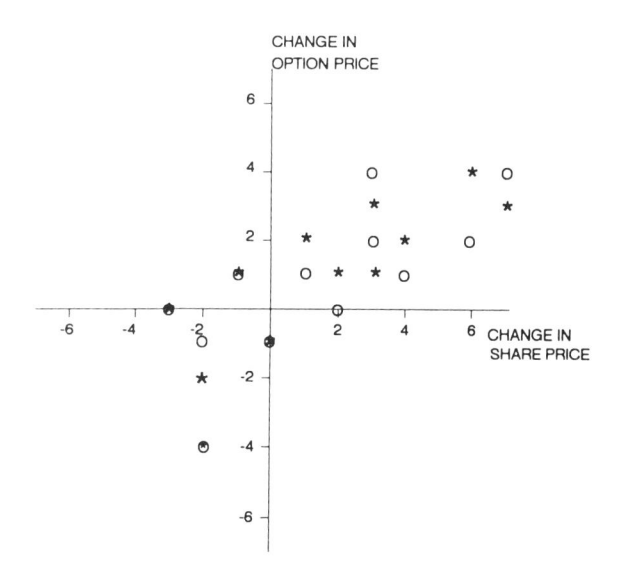

Figure 5.6. Correlation plot for British Airways April 160 (open circles) and July 160 (stars) calls.

72   TRADED OPTIONS SIMPLIFIED

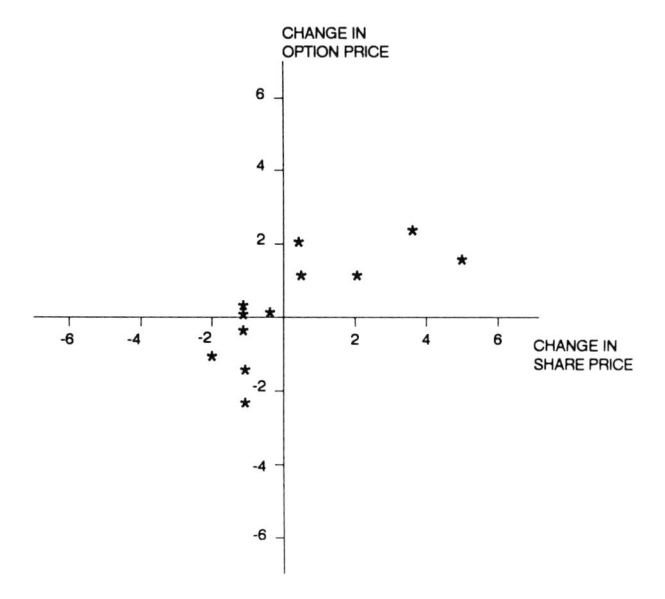

Figure 5.7. Correlation plot for British Gas April 130 calls.

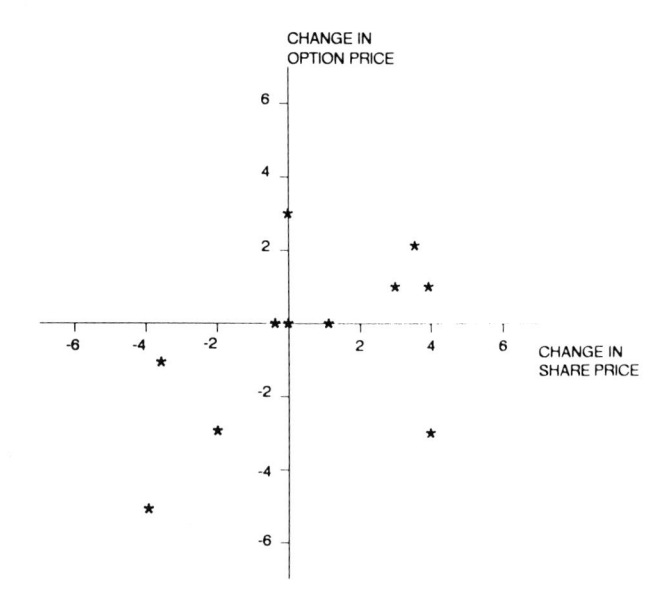

Figure 5.8. Correlation plot for BP April 260 calls.

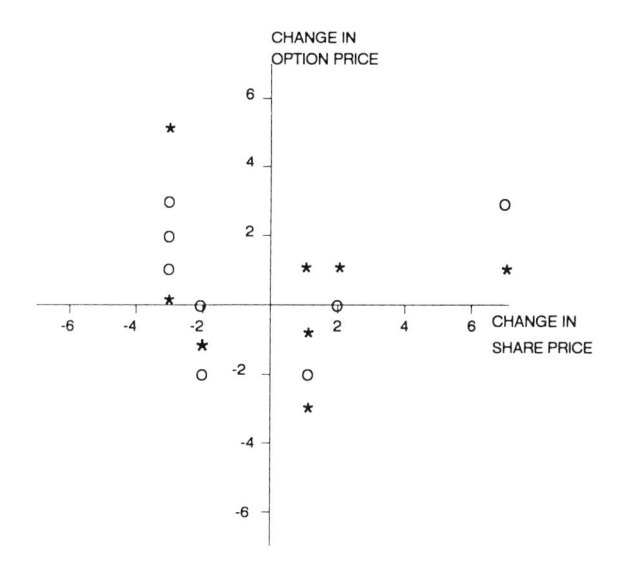

Figure 5.9. Correlation plot for Jaguar April 330 (circles) and 360 calls (stars)

Real data is plotted for several shares during a period in February 1988 in the next four figures. Figure 5.6 shows the behaviour of the British Airways April 160 calls and the British Airways July 160 calls. In both graphs the scatter about the theoretical 45 degree line is minimal, and as a yardstick for this graphical process of determining correlation, then these British Airways cases represent probably two of the best correlations that you will see. Almost as good were the British Gas April 130 calls, as shown in Figure 5.7, where again most of the points are fairly close to the 45 degree line. On the other hand the BP April 260 calls (Figure 5.8) show much more scattering, with one point very much in the - sector. Correlation is therefore poor, and BP options were to be avoided at this point in time. As an example of an extremely poor correlation, Jaguar April 330 calls and 360 calls (Figure 5.9) will take some beating. There are more points in the - and -- sectors than there are in the + and + + sectors, so that most of the time the options moved contrary to the direction of the share price. These few examples should serve to show the power and simplicity of this method of determining the degree of correlation between the share price and the option price, and the reader is urged to adopt it in order to avoid the disappointment of failing to capitalize to the maximum when the future movement of a share price has been correctly forecast.

COST PER PERCENTAGE POINT - THE WAY TO VALUE PREMIUMS

As was shown in Stocks and Shares Simplified, it is extremely important to devise methods to reduce, rapidly and virtually automatically, the vast range of investment possibilities down to a much more manageable handful. As far as traded options are concerned, we have already shown that the list can be reduced considerably by means of the concept of correlation, so that we focus on options which will behave as we expect them to behave if we have made the correct decision about the progress of the share price itself. Another consideration of vital importance is the premium associated with the particular option. The purchaser of call options (see Chapter 7) or put options (see Chapter 9) is interested in options which are cheap in terms of the premium we have to pay for a certain profit expectation. It is important that we do not confuse the actual option premium itself with what we pay for this expectation. Many beginners to traded options go for those options with the lowest premiums, in the belief that they are getting much better value for money, but have not given much consideration to the amount of risk involved with the various options. As in many other things in life, what appears cheap may well be expensive. For writers of call options (see Chapter 8) and put options (see Chapter 10), the opposite arguments will apply. The writers wish to write options as expensively (to the buyer) as possible. Thus we need a much better method than the mere value of the premium itself to determine if we are paying over the odds for call or put options, or receiving less than we should for writing call and put options for the realistic return that we may expect. A powerful way of deciding on the cost of an option is to focus on the movement of the share price required before we start to generate a profit from the premium. In order to be able to compare one share with another, we should express this movement as a percentage of the original share price. We can develop the method by referring to call options, but the ideas that we put forward here are equally applicable to put options. Having calculated the movement in share price required, we can then quite easily compare the various premiums we have to pay if purchasing, or the premium we would receive if writing options, on this logical basis. Thus an option with a high premium may only require a relatively small share price movement for profitability, whereas an option with a low premium may require a large movement. In such circumstances, the lowest premium turns out to be the most expensive of the two, since we have to take a much greater risk with our money. Conversely, the writer of the same option with a high premium may see the option exercised and the profit thereby limited. Thus quite obviously, the purchaser and the writer should be looking for opposite properties associated with the premium. The very simple way of calculating the cost per percentage point (CPP) of a call option is best

Table 5.5. Cost per Percentage Point CPP) values for call options on 12th February 1988.

Share	Striking price	Apr. prem.	Jul. prem.	Oct. prem.	Apr. CPP	Jul. CPP	Oct. CPP
Allied Lyons	300	45	50	-	15.08	11.17	-
	330	25	33	40	4.19	3.95	3.83
	360	11	22	28	1.02	1.57	1.77
British Airways	140	25	30	35	8.00	4.80	3.73
	160	13	17	24	1.60	1.60	1.60
	180	4	9	15	.27	.50	.69
Brit & Comm.	280	35	40	50	5.16	4.72	4.21
	300	22	32	37	2.40	2.55	2.60
	330	9	20	25	.60	1.07	1.23
BP	240	24	32	40	15.60	6.93	5.20
	260	11	18	28	2.60	2.60	2.60
	280	4.5	12	-	.48	.98	-
Bass	750	58	82	103	12.09	10.36	9.68
	800	32	57	78	4.04	5.11	5.62
	850	17	38	58	1.37	2.50	3.26
Cable & Wire	300	52	65	-	12.55	8.14	-
	330	30	47	57	4.61	4.07	3.93
	360	17	30	40	1.47	1.95	2.18
Cons Gold	750	100	125	140	16.00	13.33	12.44
	800	65	100	125	8.00	8.00	8.00
	850	43	85	100	3.70	5.04	5.33
Courtaulds	300	25	37	38	4.26	3.79	3.76
	330	9	23	27	.86	1.54	1.66
	360	3	15	18	.16	.68	.78
Comm Union	300	32	45	50	14.86	7.31	6.50
	330	14	28	35	2.39	2.76	2.84
	360	6	17	25	.48	1.06	1.35
British Gas	120	15	20	-	3.23	2.35	-
	130	9	14	18	1.16	1.20	1.22
	140	5	9.5	13.5	.40	.60	.71
GEC	140	18	25	26	6.93	3.50	3.34
	160	6.5	14	16	.80	1.08	1.12
	180	2	7	9	.11	.33	.40
GKN	280	29	42	48	10.91	6.02	5.35
	300	18	30	37	3.19	3.11	3.09
	330	8	18	26	.65	1.15	1.42

Table 5.5. (cont.)

Share	Striking price	Apr. prem.	Jul. prem.	Oct. prem.	Apr. CPP	Jul. CPP	Oct. CPP
Grand Met	420	42	60	68	23.84	10.48	9.08
	460	20	40	48	3.49	3.95	4.04
	500	9	21	-	.74	1.42	-
ICI	1000	77	120	135	25.98	16.96	15.87
	1050	55	95	-	9.75	10.04	-
	1100	35	77	95	4.11	6.15	6.67
Jaguar	300	35	50	60	14.31	7.11	5.95
	330	20	35	42	2.84	3.01	3.05
Land Secs	420	68	75	88	26.97	18.79	13.09
	460	38	50	65	8.22	7.00	6.31
	500	18	33	45	2.04	2.76	3.10
Marks&Spencer	160	18	24	28	3.02	2.52	2.35
	180	6	11	18	.56	.80	1.01
	200	2	7	12	.10	.30	.46
Rolls-Royce	120	12	17	22	2.14	1.77	1.62
	130	7	12	17	.73	.88	.97
	140	3.5	8	14	.24	.43	.60
STC	220	16	26	33	2.36	2.30	2.28
	240	9	16	24	.71	1.01	1.23
	260	5	12	20	.25	.52	.75
Sainsbury	200	27	33	-	8.49	5.58	-
	220	13	18	27	2.20	2.20	2.20
	240	6	12	18	.51	.83	1.04
Shell	1000	78	103	122	29.25	20.41	17.79
	1050	45	77	-	10.50	10.50	-
	1100	25	55	77	3.50	5.50	6.37
Storehouse	220	25	33	40	4.46	3.65	3.31
	240	12	23	30	1.39	1.72	1.83
	260	8	15	22	.52	.81	1.02
Trafalgar Hse	300	35	40	50	8.67	7.16	5.75
	330	17	25	35	2.19	2.44	2.62
	360	7	15	25	.50	.91	1.28
TSB	100	14	18	-	3.85	2.48	-
	110	7	13	16	1.10	1.10	1.10
	120	4	8	9	.31	.49	.52
Woolworth	240	35	38	43	5.67	5.18	4.64
	260	20	27	33	2.47	2.50	2.51
	280	15	17	23	1.08	1.16	1.35

SHARE AND OPTION PRICES 77

illustrated by reference to an example such as Trafalgar House. Thus, the necessary data for Trafalgar House call options on say 12th February 1988 is:

Share Price 322p
April 300s, 35p; April 330s, 17p; April 360s, 7p.

Taking the April 300s first, we can see that the share price has to rise to 335p (striking price + premium) before the purchase starts to move into profit. For the April 330s, the share price has to move to 347p and for the April 360s the share price has to move to 367p. Expressed as a percentage gain:

April 300s require a 13p share price rise, i.e. 4%

April 330s require a 25p share price rise, i.e. 7.8%

April 360s require a 45p share price rise, i.e. 14%.

By dividing the premium by this required percentage share price rise, we get the cost per percentage point, CPP:

April 300s = 35/4 = 8.49
April 330s = 17/7.8 = 2.19
April 360s = 7/14 = 0.5

For those who prefer a mathematical equation:

$$CPP(call) = \frac{(0.01 \times \text{premium} \times \text{share price})}{(\text{striking price} + \text{premium} - \text{share price})}$$

We can now proceed to calculate the CPPs of all the call options listed on 12th February 1988. These are given in Table 5.5, and this large amount of data allows us to determine whether there is any correlation between the cost of the option, expressed as the CPP, and the resulting price change of the shares over the course of the next few weeks. A simple way to do this is to plot a similar type of correlation diagram to those that we used earlier in this chapter. This is done in Figure 5.10, where the horizontal axis has the gain or loss in the share price by 4th March 1988, and the vertical axis has the CPPs for the in-the-money options, the values being taken from Table 5.5.

78 TRADED OPTIONS SIMPLIFIED

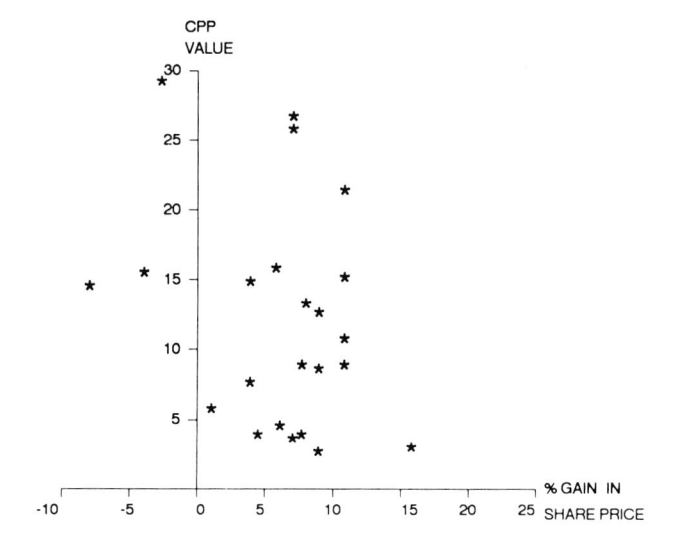

Figure 5.10. Correlation plot for gains in the share price of April in-the-money options against their CPP values.

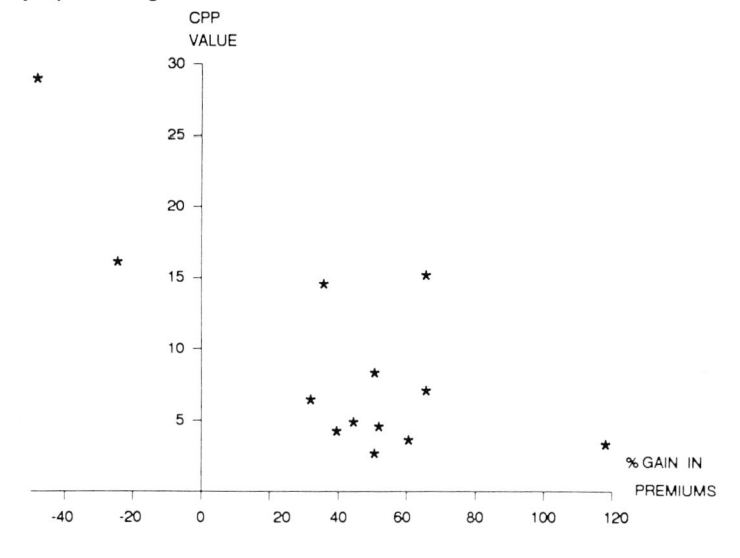

Figure 5.11. Correlation plot for gains in option prices of April in-the-money options against their CPP values.

SHARE AND OPTION PRICES   79

Table 5.6. Cost per Percentage Point (CPP) values for call options on 12th February 1988 and gain in option prices by 4th March 1988.

	Strike Price	Apr CPP	Jul CPP	Oct CPP	% Gain Apr	% Gain Jul	% Gain Oct
Allied Lyons	330	4.19	3.95	3.83	100.00	66.67	57.50
	360	1.02	1.57	1.77	127.27	59.09	60.71
British Airwys	140	8.00	4.80	3.73	64.00	43.33	34.29
	160	1.60	1.60	1.60	69.23	64.71	37.50
	180	0.27	0.50	0.69	75.00	55.56	33.33
Brit & Comm	300	2.40	2.55	2.60	45.45	31.25	35.14
	330	0.60	1.07	1.23	11.11	15.00	28.00
BP	240	15.60	6.93	5.20	-25.00	-9.38	-17.50
	260	2.60	2.60	2.60	-36.36	0.00	-17.86
	280	0.48	0.98	-	-55.56	-33.33	-
Bass	800	4.04	5.11	5.62	87.50	52.63	41.03
	850	1.37	2.50	3.26	64.71	44.74	37.93
Cable & Wrlss	330	4.61	4.07	3.93	50.00	21.28	14.04
	360	1.47	1.95	2.18	29.41	23.33	17.50
Cons Gold	800	8.00	8.00	8.00	7.69	10.00	0.00
	850	3.70	5.04	5.33	4.65	-5.88	0.00
Courtaulds	300	4.26	3.79	3.76	44.00	29.73	44.74
	330	0.86	1.54	1.66	100.00	30.43	33.33
	360	0.16	0.68	0.78	133.33	13.33	38.89
Comm Union	300	14.86	7.31	6.50	65.63	28.89	34.00
	330	2.39	2.76	2.84	7.14	7.14	14.29
	360	0.48	1.06	1.35	-16.67	-17.65	-12.00
British Gas	120	3.23	2.35	-	60.00	40.00	-
	130	1.16	1.20	1.22	61.11	42.86	22.22
	140	0.40	0.60	0.71	20.00	47.37	18.52
GEC	140	6.93	3.50	3.34	33.33	20.00	15.38
	160	0.80	1.08	1.12	23.08	14.29	12.50
	180	0.11	0.33	0.40	0.00	14.29	11.11
GKN	300	3.19	3.11	3.09	138.89	60.00	43.24
	330	0.65	1.15	1.42	100.00	72.22	53.85
Grand Met	460	3.49	3.95	4.04	175.00	87.50	77.08
	500	0.74	1.42	-	200.00	123.81	-
ICI	1050	9.75	10.04	-	30.91	21.05	-
	1100	4.11	6.15	6.67	28.57	14.29	21.05
Jaguar	300	14.31	7.11	5.95	34.29	10.00	13.33
	330	2.84	3.01	3.05	10.00	5.71	19.05

80 TRADED OPTIONS SIMPLIFIED

Figure 5.6. (cont.)

Land Secs	460	8.22	7.00	6.31	63.16	44.00	27.69
	500	2.04	2.76	3.10	77.78	36.36	33.33
Marks & Spencer	160	3.02	2.52	2.35	38.89	25.00	14.29
	180	0.56	0.80	1.01	50.00	63.64	16.67
	200	0.10	0.30	0.46	0.00	28.57	8.33
Rolls-Royce	120	2.14	1.77	1.62	50.00	29.41	22.73
	130	0.73	0.88	0.97	42.86	33.33	23.53
	140	0.24	0.43	0.60	28.57	31.25	14.29
STC	220	2.36	2.30	2.28	125.00	76.92	51.52
	240	0.71	1.01	1.23	88.89	93.75	58.33
	260	0.25	0.52	0.75	20.00	66.67	35.00
Sainsbury	220	2.20	2.20	2.20	100.00	66.67	25.93
	240	0.51	0.83	1.04	83.33	33.33	16.67
Shell	1000	29.25	20.41	17.79	-52.60	-32.04	-28.69
	1050	10.50	10.50	-	-96.63	-38.96	-
	1100	3.50	5.50	6.37	-72.00	-50.91	-35.06
Storehouse	220	4.46	3.65	3.31	52.00	36.36	17.50
	240	1.39	1.72	1.83	91.67	21.74	16.67
	260	0.52	0.81	1.02	25.00	20.00	13.64
Trafalgar House	300	8.67	7.16	5.75	51.43	42.50	30.00
	330	2.19	2.44	2.62	64.71	48.00	37.14
	360	0.50	0.91	1.28	57.14	46.67	32.00
TSB	100	3.85	2.48	-	35.71	22.22	-
	110	1.10	1.10	1.10	71.43	23.08	12.50
	120	0.31	0.49	0.52	25.00	12.50	33.33
Woolworth	280	1.08	1.16	1.35	100.00	117.65	86.95

It becomes obvious from the correlation diagram that the shares whose options had the most expensive CPPs gave no better return during the following few weeks than those whose options had inexpensive CPPs. The same conclusion would be reached for the out-of-the-money options. Before deciding that the obvious message is that as purchasers we should stick with those options which have the lower CPPs, we should carry out the same exercise to see if there is any correlation between CPPs and the gain (or loss) which would be made in the options themselves, since of course it is the gain in the option premiums which interest the purchaser of traded options. The results of the calculation for these gains are given in Table 5.6.

A correlation diagram for the gains in the April in-the-money options against the CPP values, is shown in Figure 5.11. Again, it is obvious that there is no correlation between CPP and the gain to be made in the option, and although these are not shown, correlation diagrams for the other out-of-the-money options give the same uncompromising message. Out of the 14 options plotted in the diagram, the seven with the highest CPPs (averaging 13.9) gave an average gain of 24.4% over the period, while those seven with the lowest CPPs (averaging 3.03) gave an average gain of 68.4%. Looked at another way, the purchaser of the top seven CPP options would have put at risk four times as much money (as a cost per percentage gain) and achieved only a third of the gain of the investor in the bottom seven CPP options and therefore is a factor of twelve worse off in terms of achievement per CPP. This is not just an aberration during the period from February to March 1988. The same general type of results are obtained from any period of time since the beginning of the Traded Options market in London and is applicable to out-of-the-money options as well as in-the-money options. The message is quite clear: purchasers should avoid those options which fall into the top half of the league table of CPP values and concentrate on those in the bottom half. The writers of call options, as we shall see in Chapter 8, take a completely opposite view of premiums. While the purchaser is wishing to keep the premium, expressed as a CPP, as low as possible, the writer wishes to receive as high a premium as possible against the risk that the share price will rise. The purchaser is interested in the gain in the premium itself, but the writer is interested in the premium falling to zero by the time the option expires, so that it is not exercised against him. Because of this fact, the writer should be looking closely at the relationship between CPP values and the ensuing change in the share price. Since we drew the conclusion earlier that there was no advantage for a purchaser in buying options with high CPPs, then high CPP options must give an advantage to the writer. The advantage is that these options provide a return, in terms of the premium received, which is as high as possible for the degree of risk which is being accepted by the writer. This aspect is covered more fully in Chapter 8. The points which have been made about call options and CPP values apply in exactly the same way to put options. The purchaser of put options should be seeking those options where the CPPs are lowest, while the writer of puts should be writing those options where the CPPs are highest. However, note that CPPs for put options are calculated in a different way from those for call options and refer to the cost per percentage point fall that the share price has to undergo before the position becomes profitable. As an example, Trafalgar House had these values for put options on 12th February 1988:

Share price 322p: April 300s, 8p; April 330s, 20p and April 360s, 43p.

Taking the April 300s first, we can see that the share price has to fall to 292p (striking price - premium) before the purchaser starts to move into profit. For the April 330s, the share price has to move to 310p and for the April 360s the share price has to move to 317p. Expressed as a percentage fall:

April 300s require a 30p (322p - 292p) price fall, i.e. 9.31%
April 330s require a 12p (322p - 310p) price fall, i.e. 3.72%
April 360s require a 5p (322p - 317p) price fall, i.e. 1.55%

By dividing the premium by this required percentage share price fall, we get the cost per percentage point, CPP for the put option:

April 300s = 8/9.31 = 0.859
April 330s = 20/3.72 = 5.376
April 360s = 43/1.55 = 27.742

Compare these with the CPP values of the corresponding call options calculated previously:

April 300s = 8.49
April 330s = 2.19
April 360s = 0.5

The inverse relationship follows because at a share price of 322p, the April 300 call options are in-the-money, while the April 300 put options are out-of-the-money. Thus CPP values are high for in-the-money call and put options and low for out-of-the-money call and put options.

The equation for a put option (compare with that for the call option given earlier) is:

$$\text{CPP(put option)} = \frac{(0.01 \times \text{premium} \times \text{share price})}{(\text{share price} + \text{premium} - \text{share price})}$$

Finally, the discussion in this chapter shows that by taking note of the concept of correlation, both between share price and option premiums and between cost per percentage point and option premiums, the very large number of available options can be reduced to a mere handful, say about six classes. This considerably simplifies the task of selecting which option will be the vehicle for investment, where the other consideration, addressed in the remaining chapters, will revolve around the degree of risk which the investor is prepared to accept.

CHAPTER 6

Option Strategies

There are two main categories of investor active in the Traded Options market. There are those who wish to make a profit out of an anticipated movement in the price of the underlying security, and there are those who wish to insure an existing portfolio against an adverse market move by taking out an option position to cover this eventuality. If there is any difference between these two categories of investor, it is probably that the first category has a more positive feeling about the direction of the market. The second category, like a person taking out house insurance, hopes that the worst will not happen, but knows that at least he will be compensated if it does. He is therefore less positive that the market will move against him, because of course if he was surer about the future course of events he could adjust the portfolio by selling or buying as appropriate.

Whichever category of investor we consider, their reason for involvement in the Traded Options market at a particular time is because they have come to some conclusion about the probable behaviour of the market in general or a share in particular in the near future. They may have used techniques such as those discussed in Chapters 3 and 4; they may have some information whose significance the general public has not yet come to appreciate; or they may just have a hunch about the likely course of events.

These future events can follow only three paths:

1. The share price/market will rise.
2. The share price/market will fall.
3. The share price/market will stay more or less constant.

Investors will naturally hold one of the above views of the direction of a share price or the market in the immediate future. These investors can obviously be described as bulls, bears or neutrals respectively. If they restrict their activities to the normal share market, then only the bulls can make a good profit. Because of the limited opportunity for short selling (i.e. selling a share before you have bought it) in the UK market, bears would have to rely on a drastic fall in price within the account period or over two account periods in order to make

84 TRADED OPTIONS SIMPLIFIED

a profit after covering the costs of the transaction. The neutral investor would make no profit at all. By turning to the Traded Options market, each of these types of investor can make a profit, provided he has taken the correct view of the future movement of the underlying share price.

Within each of these categories of investor, there will be different shades of opinion as to the certainty that events will unfold as predicted. There will be different shades of opinion as to the extent of any rises or falls, and in the case of neutrals, the upper and lower limits within which the price will move in the future. As will be shown in this Chapter, there will be an optimum strategy for each of these various shades of opinion.

CATERING FOR SHADES OF OPINION

Investors in traded options have four simple routes open to them, and may combine several of these simple routes into increasingly complex strategies, some of the latter being so complex that a great deal of mathematics has to be applied.

These simple routes involve the buying or selling of simple call options and the buying or selling of simple put options:

Call options:
buyers expect a rise in share price.
sellers ("writers") do not expect the share price to rise significantly.

Put options:
buyers expect a share price fall.
writers do not expect the share price to fall significantly.

Even neglecting complex mixed strategies, the above four routes can cause confusion. The reader may come to the conclusion that the buyer of a call option and the writer of a put option are expecting the same outcome, viz. a rise in the share price. Conversely it might appear that the buyer of a put option and the writer of a call option expect a fall in the share price. While it is true that a call option buyer and put option writer will both profit from a share price rise, and a put option buyer and call option writer will both profit from a share price fall, the put option and call option writers can profit from a share price standstill while the others cannot. Therefore, quite obviously, there are subtle and not-so-subtle differences in their expectations, and these differences will become more apparent when we discuss the question of risk. The whole thrust of investing in traded options is that the degree of risk taken on board can be tailored, using either simple or complex strategies, to the degree of certainty in the mind of the investor as to the future movement in the price of the underlying security.

Degrees of Risk

Taking a very simplified view, the various strategies discussed in the remainder of this book can be listed in order of decreasing risk as follows:

High Risk: writing uncovered call options
writing covered calls
writing puts
writing straddles

Medium Risk: buying call options
buying put options

Low Risk: bull spreads
bear spreads
calendar spreads
buying straddles

A more exact analysis of the risk/reward position for each strategy will be undertaken in the appropriate chapter, but Table 6.1. shows in simple terms the risk and reward associated with each strategy.

Table 6.1. Reward and Risk for various option strategies.

Strategy	Reward	Risk	Chapter
Buy calls	unlimited	limited	7
Write covered calls	limited	unlimited	8
Write uncovered calls	limited	unlimited	8
Buy puts	unlimited	limited	9
Write puts	limited	unlimited	10
Bull spread	limited	limited	11
Bear spread	limited	limited	11
Calendar spread	limited	limited	11
Buy straddle	unlimited	limited	12
Write straddle	limited	unlimited	12

Covered options are those where the underlying shares are also held, ence the writer of a covered call option can supply the shares if the option is called (exercised) by the buyer. The writer of an uncovered option does not hold the shares and therefore if called will have to buy them in the market to supply the caller.

The above view of the various possibilities is simplified, since the amount of risk implicit in any of the strategies will depend upon the expiry dates and striking prices of the options involved. As will be seen later, the amount of risk within one of the above strategies can be adjusted as required by the circumstances. Therefore it is, as an example, possible to open a spread position where the risk is high and not low as listed above.

What might appear paradoxical is the fact that the simplest option strategies to understand, i.e. the buying of a call or a put option, are not those with the lowest risk, but this becomes apparent as we discuss the risk associated with each strategy more fully.

Writing uncovered call options

These are profitable if the share price falls, remains static, or shows only a very small rise. The degree of tolerance to a small rise depends upon the extent to which the option is out-of-the- money. The investor has almost unlimited exposure in the event of a sharp upwards price movement due for instance to a takeover bid. He will have to buy a similar option to offset the one he has written, and may well have to pay a large multiple of the original cost in order to do this. Alternatively the call may be exercised against him and he will have to buy the shares in the market at a price well above the strike price in order to supply the buyer of the option. Note that the call can be exercised at any time, and therefore the writer is in a situation over which he has very little control.

Writing Put Options

These are profitable only if the share price rises, remains static, or shows a very small fall. In the latter case, the extent of the fall which can be tolerated depends upon the degree to which the option is out-of-the-money. The investor has a high exposure in the event of a sharp fall. Although this is limited to the difference between the striking price and the share price, the potential loss is very high since (in theory anyway) the share price can fall all the way to zero. Again, as with call options, the option can be exercised against the writer at any time, the writer having no control over this.

Buying Call and Put Options

Here there is only a profit if the share price rises (call options) or falls (put options). The loss is limited to the amount of premium that has been paid although this can vary from a small amount, say £20 per contract up to a much larger amount, say £1000 per contract.

Writing Covered Calls

These are profitable if the share price falls, remains static or shows a very small rise. The degree of tolerance to a small rise depends upon the extent to which the option is out-of-the-money. In the event of a price rise the buyer may exercise the option. The real loss then will be the difference between the share price and the strike price, less any premiums received. The loss may turn out to be relatively small.

Complex Strategies

These strategies involve the buying or writing of at least two different options, and therefore the loss usually involves the difference between two premiums, which is usually comparatively small. However, some strategies could lead to the loss of two premiums and hence involve higher risk than the buying of simple call and put options.

It is helpful at this stage to subdivide further the bull, bear and neutral categories. This can be done either from the degree of certainty they feel about their view of the future security price, or from whether they think a price rise, price fall or the price band within which prices will move will be small, medium or large.

Categories of Investor

The degree of risk which an investor is prepared to carry should be in direct proportion to the certainty he has about the future course of the particular share price in which he is interested. Since the above strategies were collated with their associated risk, it is therefore possible to correlate the strategy the

Table 6.2. Option strategies for various views of share price movement.

Bullish	Buy call
	Bull spread
	Calendar spread
	Write put
	Write covered call
Bearish	Buy put
	Bear spread
	Calendar spread
	Write uncovered call
Neutral	Write straddle
	Calendar spread
Non-neutral	Write straddle

investor should employ with his view about the share price. This is done in Table 6.2.

Within these strategies there are of course varying degrees of risk, so that a bullish investor can select the appropriate strategy for his circumstances. Within each strategy there are once again varying degrees of risk, so that the investor can really fine-tune his selection.

The non-neutral category is the one that covers the situation where the investor does not expect the price to remain stable, but has no idea whether the price will rise or fall. Although rarely employed, it can be used to cover the case where a share with a volatile history has traded within a narrow range for some time. Chartists would expect a break-out from this range within a certain time, and therefore can cover themselves with this strategy. The author's view is that since there are such a large number of shares for which traded options are available, then by using the techniques discussed in Chapters 3 and 4 it is always possible to find a share about which you can be much more positive about the direction and extent of its price movement.

CHAPTER 7

Buying Call Options

A call option gives the buyer of the option the right to buy a number, usually 1000, shares of the underlying security at a fixed price - the striking price - at any time up to the expiry date of the option. The purchase of call options is the strategy for investors with bullish expectations for the particular share price, and this strategy is attended by a moderate amount of risk. The purchaser expects the value of the option to rise as the share price rises, but also expects a high degree of gearing, i.e. the increase in the value of the option, expressed as a percentage, is very much greater than the increase in the value of the underlying shares over the same period of time. Within the bounds of normal behaviour of share prices and option prices, the holder of a call option has an almost unlimited potential for gain, while his potential for loss is limited solely to the premium he has paid for the option, plus the expenses involved in the deal.

A major attraction of call options is that the buyer can select from a variety of options, thereby tailoring the amount of risk he is prepared to accept to his own particular psychological and financial circumstances. By and large the profit potential will be proportional to the amount of risk which is accepted, although, as is shown in the chapter, it is possible to find options which have lower premiums than expected. These will provide a lower risk vehicle for the more astute investor.

Limited Loss, Unlimited Gain

The profit or loss potential of a call option at the expiry date can be plotted as a function of the share price at expiry to give a graph of characteristic shape as shown in Figure 7.1. The point A shown on the share price axis represents the striking price. Obviously at any value below this there is a total loss of the premium, hence the horizontal line. This is of course the maximum loss that can be sustained. As the share price rises, the loss gets less until at point B the option value is the same as the original premium paid, and the loss then becomes zero. It is only above this point B that the position moves into profit. Note however that the profit continues upwards as a sloping line, i.e. there is essentially no upper limit. In practice of course there is some limit since share

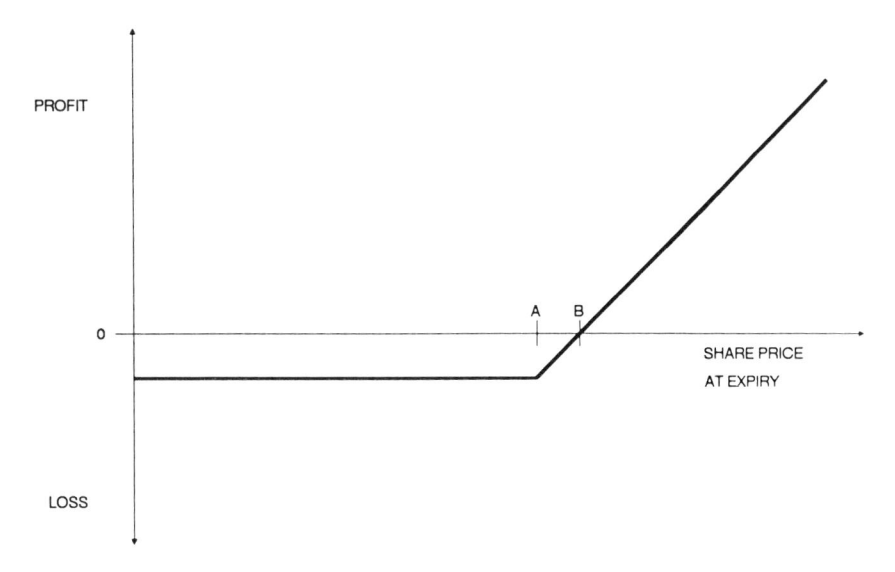

Figure 7.1. Profit/loss potential of a call option for different share prices at expiry time.

prices do not rise to an infinite level, but there are many instances, e.g. due to takeover bids, that they can rise to very high levels extremely rapidly.

The graph illustrates the major attribute of the purchase of call options in that the loss is limited while the gain is unlimited. Actual values have been left off the axes in Figure 7.1, because the purpose is to convey the shape of the graph and the concept of limited loss, unlimited gain. Values can be put on the axes depending upon the premium paid and the extent to which the options are in-the-money or out-of-the-money.

Option Premiums

Table 7.1 shows the premiums for various call options on 26th February 1988, one class being taken from each of the three available time cycles. Two points which are of general application, irrespective of which companies' shares being considered, can be illustrated by the data in Table 7.1:

1. The least expensive option is always the nearest expiry, furthest out-of-the-money, e.g. Dixons March 220s, Trafalgar House April 360s and British Telecom May 260s.

2. The most expensive option is always the furthest expiry, deepest in-the-money, e.g. Dixons September 180s, Trafalgar House October 300s and British Telecom November 220s.

Table 7.1. Premiums for Various Call Options on 26th February 1988.

Share	Price	Option	Expiry Date and Premium		
Dixons	187	180	[MAR]12	[JUN]22	[SEP]27
		200	3	12	17
		220	1.5	6	12
Trafalgar House	329	300	[APR]38	[JUL]45	[OCT]52
		330	18	27	35
		360	7	14	25
British Telecom	244	220	[MAY]30	[AUG]36	[NOV]41
		240	16	21	29
		260	6.5	12	17

A perusal of any table of option premiums in the quality newspapers will establish that these two observations are always true. The reason that the nearest expiry, furthest out-of-the-money options are cheapest is because they have no intrinsic value, and there is very little time left for an upward share price movement to put them in-the-money at expiry day. The opposite is true for the most expensive option. These have the highest intrinsic values, since they are furthest in-the-money, and in addition they have plenty of time left for the share price to make an upward move to add to their value.

This is about as far as we can go in generalising from one class of options to another. The April 300 option premium for one share for example is unlikely to be the same as the premium for the April 300 premium for another share. Even if by chance they were the same, you would find a difference in say the July 300s. This is because investors will have different perceptions of the volatility of the particular share price and the direction of the trend. What we can do however is generalise about the behaviour of option prices within an option class, based upon logical analysis of premiums in terms of their intrinsic values and time values. Such an analysis will guide us in the choice of the best option for the particular circumstances, since we can achieve a firmer grasp of the risk and reward associated with the various option series.

Relationship between Premiums and Share price

In deciding to buy any type of call option, the investor will have made reasoned decisions as to the extent to which the share price will rise, and also the timescale over which this will happen. This will have been done by using the principles discussed in Chapters 3 and 4. The best insight into the

92 TRADED OPTIONS SIMPLIFIED

relationship between the option prices and the share price is to consider the case where the price movement upwards is expected to occur over the short time between the purchase of the option and the nearest expiry date. Three scenarios can be envisaged:

1. The share price remains static - the RISK
2. An upward share price movement occurs - the REWARD
3. The share price falls - the RISK

Since all premiums are composed of an intrinsic value (which might be zero) and a time value, the effect on these of each of the above three outcomes can be discussed, thus giving a picture of the overall effect on the option premium.

Intrinsic Values

Because of the mathematical fact that intrinsic values are the difference between the share price and the striking price, if positive, then the following will be true:

1. Static price movement will leave intrinsic values unchanged.

2. Upward share price movement will increase intrinsic values on a penny for penny basis, and some options with zero intrinsic value will move into a state of positive intrinsic value as the movement continues.

3. Downward price movement will decrease intrinsic values on a penny for penny basis, and some options will move to zero intrinsic value as the movement continues.

The theoretical effect of an upward share price movement on call options which initially have no intrinsic value (because the share price is below the striking price) is shown in Figure 7.2(a). At some point the upward price movement takes the share price past the striking price, at which point the graph takes on a slope of 45 degrees, i.e. the increase is on a penny for penny basis.

The effect of a downward movement on call options which initially do have an intrinsic value is shown in Figure 7.2(b). Here the graph falls at a slope of 45 degrees due to the penny for penny fall in the intrinsic value with share price. Once the share price becomes equal to the striking price, the intrinsic value becomes zero and remains so with further fall in share price.

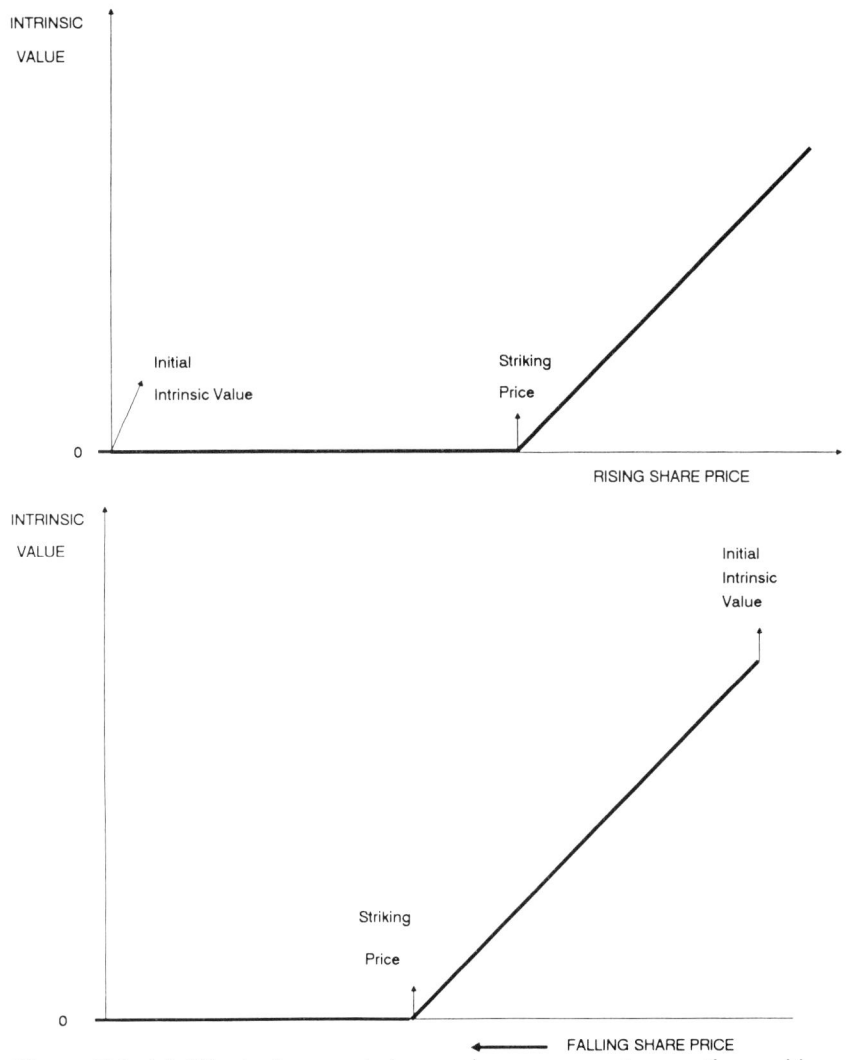

Figure 7.2. (a) Effect of upward share price movement on options with no initial intrinsic value (b) Effect of downward price movement on shares which have initial intrinsic value.

Time Values

The situation with intrinsic value is of course perfectly straightforward, because intrinsic values are simply the difference between the share price and the striking price, if this difference is positive. Time values are not based upon

94   TRADED OPTIONS SIMPLIFIED

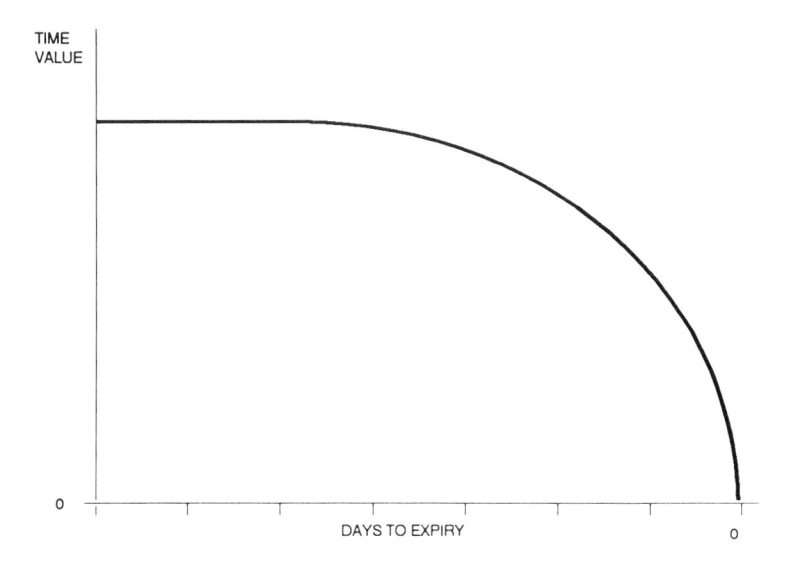

Figure 7.3. Loss of time value of an option up to expiry time, assuming share price remains constant.

such a mathematical relationship, but on what investors think will happen to the share price over the period of time remaining to expiry. Depending upon the date at which a snapshot view is taken, this time can vary from a day to nine months. As a rough guide, the following reactions might be expected:

1. A static share price should not have a positive effect on time values, and as stated above, normal behaviour under such circumstances is for the time value to fall rapidly during the last six weeks or so of the life of the option, becoming zero at expiry.

2. An upward price movement should have a positive effect on time values, with the greatest effect being on the more distant expiry dates. Since time values where the share price remains constant tend to decrease during the last month or two of the life of an option, becoming zero at expiry, the positive effect of the upward share price movement should cancel this normal decrease, leaving options with say two to eight weeks lifetime virtually unchanged. Options with very little time left to expiry should still exhibit the normal decrease unless a very substantial share price rise occurs to cancel out the disappearing time value.

3. A downward price movement should have most effect on the time values of those options of nearest expiry, causing these to fall even more rapidly than in the static share price case. This is because investors should see that there is very little

Table 7.2. Movement of Dixons Share and Call Option Prices from 12/2/88 to 11/3/88 (Time Values in [ ])

Item		12/2/88	19/2/88	27/2/88	4/3/88	11/3/88
Share Price		180	187	187	185	184
MAR	180s	12[12]	12[5]	12 [5]	11[6]	7 [3]
	200s	5[5]	4[4]	3[3]	3[3]	1[1]
	220s	2[2]	2[2]	1.5[1.5]	1[1]	1[1]
JUN	180s	20[20]	23[16]	22[15]	23[18]	20[16]
	200s	12[12]	13[13]	12[12]	11[11]	11[11]
	220s	6[6]	7[7]	6[6]	6[6]	6[6]
SEP	180s	28[28]	28[[21]	27[20]	28[23]	28[24]
	200s	18[18]	19[19]	17[17]	18[18]	19[19]
	220s	11[11]	13[13]	12[12]	12[18]	11 [11]

time left for the adverse trend to reverse itself. Options with more distant expiry dates should see their time values remain more or less constant unless the share price fall becomes substantial, in which case time values will be eroded.

These various cases are best illustrated by means of examples, and these examples will also serve to underline the very approximate nature of the above comments, since they must not be taken as rigid rules which will apply in every situation. There will always be many anomalies. Very often these anomalies can provide situations which can be exploited for improved profit, provided that the investor is correct about his fundamental view of the future share price movement.

The least approximate case, and therefore the one case which can be represented graphically, is the one where the share price remains more or less constant over the last weeks before expiry of the option. This is shown in Figure 7.3.

1. Static Share Prices - Dixons and Thorn-EMI Call Options

The most useful example to analyse in order to understand more clearly the relationship between share prices and options prices is the case where the share price remains more or less static. Two such examples, at fairly widely separated dates, will serve for this purpose.

96 TRADED OPTIONS SIMPLIFIED

Table 7.3. Movement of Thorn-EMI Share and Call Option Prices from 8/1/88 to 5/2/88 (Time Values in [ ])

Item		8/1/88	15/1/88	22/1/88	30/1/88	5/2/88
Share Price		564	572	570	574	567
MAR	500s	87[23]	90[18]	87[17]	90[16]	82[15]
	550s	50[34]	60[38]	52[32]	55[31]	44[27]
	600s	25[25]	30[30]	28[28]	25[25]	18[18]
JUN	500s	110[46]	113[41]	10[40]	113[39]	100[32]
	550s	77[61]	80[58]	80[60]	82[58]	73[56]
	600s	50[50]	53[53]	53[53]	55[55]	48[48]
SEP	500s	120[56]	130[58]	120[50]	125[51]	117[50]
	550s	80[66]	95[73]	97[77]	95[71]	87[70]
	600s	60[60]	67[67]	67[67]	67[67]	60[60]

Table 7.4. Movement of Thorn-EMI Share and Call Option Prices from 12/2/88 to 11/3/88 (Time Values in [ ])

Item		12/2/88	19/2/88	26/2/88	4/3/88	11/3/88
Share Price		554	561	567	598	604
MAR	550s	32[28]	29[18]	30[19]	54[6]	57[3]
	600s	9[9]	9[9]	[77]	1[11]	10[6]
JUN	550s	60[54]	55[44]	57[60]	77[29]	82[28]
	600s	33[33]	32[32]	32[32]	45[45]	46[42]
SEP	550s	65 [61]	67[56]	70[53]	85[37]	97[43]
	600s	45[45]	43[43]	42[42]	55 [55]	62 [58]

Between 12th February and 11th March 1988 the Dixons share price moved in narrow limits of 180p to 187p, ending at 184p. Table 7.2 shows the movement of the various option premiums over the same time period.

The prediction above was that a static share price would lead to static option premiums, except for those near to expiry, which would should a rapid erosion of time values. Table 7.2 shows this prediction to be fairly close to reality, with the near term March options falling rapidly as time values (shown in square brackets) diminish. Longer term options show either modest or zero falls in time values, so that the overall premiums remain virtually static.

The Dixons case covered a situation where the short term options had only two weeks to go to expiry date, where we expect therefore a fall in time values of the short term options. For a case where the nearest expiry date for an option is still two months away, we would expect all premiums to remain more or less static due to stable time values. Although the Thorn-EMI share price remained just about stationary between 8/1/88 and 5/2/88, the option premiums did not behave quite as expected, as shown by the data given in Table 7.3.

The September premiums did stay more or less static, as did the June 550s and 600s, but the June 500s and all of the short term March options showed considerable falls in their time values, even though there were two more months remaining. Note also, and this appears to apply in general to all options, that time values are highest for those options which are closest to being at-the-money. These comments show the major difficulty with options in that any "rules" we make are extremely empirical, and must only be used in the context of being very general guidelines. The interesting question that might be asked is of course whether buyers of the short expiry Thorn-EMI options were correct in their view that the share price would rise significantly.

As can be seen from the data in Table 7.4, such investors were correct. The price did rise by nearly 10% over the following five weeks giving an excellent response with March 550s. An interesting aspect of this set of data is the erosion of the time values for both June and September 550s, while the June and September 600s show an increase in time values. This has to be considered anomalous behaviour, and makes the 550 options attractive against the 600 options for the relatively conservative investor.

2. Rising Share Price - Courtaulds and Trafalgar House

As buyers of call options, expecting the share price to rise, then naturally we are much more interested in what happens when the price rises than when it falls or remains the same. In order to gain as much information as possible about the effect on option premiums of a rising share price, it is useful to compare two shares which made similar gains and had fairly comparable prices over a short period of time. Such a pair is Courtaulds and Trafalgar House, which both made gains of about 8% between February 12th and March 4th 1988. Courtaulds started at 307p while Trafalgar House started at 322p. On any simple view, we would therefore expect their options to behave fairly similarly. However, remembering our discussion about correlation, we would only expect similar behaviour of the option prices if both shares showed a high correlation between share price and option price. However, the correlation for Courtaulds is poor, while that for Trafalgar House, while not excellent, is good. This simply reinforces our earlier view that the relationship between share

98   TRADED OPTIONS SIMPLIFIED

Table 7.5. Movement of Courtaulds Share and Call Option Prices from 12/2/88 to 11/3/88 (Time Values in [ ])

Item		12/2/88	19/2/88	26/2/88	4/3/88	11/3/88
Share Price		307	302	312	331	317
APR	300s	25[18]	18[16]	25[13]	36[5]	27[10]
	330s	9[9]	8[8]	11[11]	18[17]	10[10]
	360s	3[3]	3[3]	4[4]	7[7]	2[2]
JUL	300s	37[30]	32[30]	35[23]	48[17]	38[21]
	330s	23[23]	20[20]	18[18]	30[29]	46[46]
	360s	15[15]	12[12]	10[10]	17[17]	12[12]
OCT	300s	38[31]	35[33]	43[31]	55[24]	45[28]
	330s	27[27]	25[25]	25[25]	36[35]	22[22]
	360s	18[18]	15[15]	18[18]	25[25]	18[18]

Table 7.6. Movement of Trafalgar House Share and Call Option Prices from 12/2/88 to 11/3/88 (Time Values in [ ])

Item		12/2/88	19/2/88	26/2/88	4/3/88	11/3/88
Share price		322	317	329	346	325
APR	300s	35[13]	30[13]	38[8]	53[7]	33 [8]
	330s	17[17]	13[13]	18[18]	28[12]	15[15]
	360s	7[7]	5[5]	7[7]	11[11]	5[5]
JUL	300s	40[18]	37[20]	45[16]	57[11]	40[15]
	330s	25[25]	22[22]	27[27]	37[21]	23[23]
	360s	15[15]	15[15]	14[14]	22[22]	13[13]
OCT	300s	50[28]	47[30]	52[23]	65[19]	52[27]
	330s	35[35]	32[19]	35[35]	48[32]	35[35]
	360s	25[25]	22[22]	25[25]	33[33]	23[23]

Table 7.7. Movement of Standard Telephone & Cables (STC) Share and Call Option Prices from 12/2/88 to 11/3/88 (Time Values in [ ])

Item		12/2/88	19/2/88	26/2/88	4/3/88	11/3/88
Share price		221	232	243	256	247
APR	220s	16 [15]	21[9]	25[2]	36[0]	28[1]
	240s	9[9]	12[12]	6[13]	7[1]	15[8]
	260s	5[5]	6[6]	8[8]	6[6]	5[5]
JUL	220s	26[25]	31[19]	38[25]	46[10]	38[11]
	240s	16[16]	19[19]	24[21]	31[15]	25[18]
	260s	12[12]	13[13]	18[18]	20[20]	14[14]
OCT	220s	33[32]	37[25]	43[20]	50[14]	44[17]
	240s	24[24]	29[29]	33[30]	38[22]	33[26]
	260s	20[20]	22[22]	24[24]	27[27]	24[24]

Table 7.8. General conclusions on the effect of share price rise on time values and intrinsic values of call options. Percentages are average values from Courtaulds, Trafalgar House and STC between 12/2/88 and 4/3/88.

Type of option	Effect on intrinsic value	Effect on time value
Short term in-the-money	rise	very large fall (-72%)
Short term out-of-the-money	stays zero	good rise (+70%)
Medium term in-the-money	rise	large fall (-58%)
Medium term out-of-the money	stays zero	modest rise (+42%)
Long term in-the-money	rise	modest fall (-37%)
Long term out-of-the-money	stays zero	modest rise (+35%)

price and option price is not a rigid one. To see the effect of a larger rise than these two shares experienced, we also include data for STC, where the rise was about double this 8%.

Table 7.9. Movement of Woolworth Share and Call Option Prices from 20/11/87 to 18/12/87 (Time Values in [ ])

Item		20/11/87	27/11/87	4/12/87	11/12/87	18/12/87
Share price:		287	269	240	261	239
JAN	280s	30[23]	20[20]	6 [6]	9 [9]	4 [4]
APR	280s	50[43]	50[50]	20[20]	25[25]	15[15]
JUL	280s	55[48]	65[65]	25[25]	30[30]	20[20]

Our earlier general prediction from first principles was that an upward share price movement may have the effect of turning a zero intrinsic value into a positive one, and also have a positive effect on time values, being greatest on the more distant expiry dates, and probably causing the nearest ones to remain steady rather than experience their normal fall. While the predictions were naturally correct for intrinsic value, since that is simply a mathematical relationship, they were totally incorrect as far as time values are concerned. What becomes immediately obvious from Tables 7.5 to 7.7 is that there is a interaction between intrinsic value and time value. During the period of the rise in share prices (12/2/88 to 4/3/88) only options which stayed out-of-the-money, i.e. had zero intrinsic values, which showed a rise in time values. In-the-money options with intrinsic values exhibit a fall in time values. Where there are rises in time values, the more distant expiry dates seem to enjoy less of a rise than sometimes the middle term and sometimes the near term expiring options.

Table 7.10. Expected gains, on a scale of 1 to 5, for various categories of call options.

in-the-money	+ + +	+ +	+
at-the-money	+ + + +	+ + +	+ +
out-of-the-money	+ + + + +	+ + + +	+ + +
	short expiry	medium expiry	long expiry

We can now attempt to draw some general conclusions about the behaviour of intrinsic values and time values of options where the underlying share price has risen, before moving on to the implications for potential profit/risk.

3. Falling Share Price - Woolworths

Earlier it was pointed out that the most marked effect on premiums where the share price falls over a month or so should be on the time values of the nearest expiry option. In addition, those options which are in-the-money could become out-of-the-money, and hence lose all their intrinsic value. The net result should be a rapid erosion of the short term premiums and a rather less rapid erosion of the longer expiry options.

The data for Woolworth in Table 7.9 supports the expected reaction perfectly. The time values of the nearest January options deteriorated from 23 to 4 (82% loss) in a matter of four weeks, while the next longer expiry April options time values fell from 43 to 15 (65% loss) and the longest July options time values fell from 48 to 20 (58% loss).

Potential for Profit and Loss

The foregoing discussion of intrinsic values and time values for falling, rising and static share prices is intended to give a background against which investors can select the correct option for the degree of risk and the potential reward that they require. As a result of the correlation approach discussed in Chapter 5, we are now of course faced with a greatly reduced number of options from which to choose. This reduced list of options has to be considered in the light of the two important dimensions - the gap between the actual share price and the striking price (i.e. the extent to which the option is in- or out-of-the-money), and the length of time to expiry (i.e. short, medium or long).

Just to give an approximate idea of the potential gains, we can consider a matrix containing nine boxes, with one pair of opposite sides representing the gap between striking price and share price and the other pair of sides the length of time to expiry. The gains made from a rise in share price are shown on a scale of 1 to 5. It must be stressed that this is approximate, and there will often be exceptions, but the diagram (Table 7.10) will be helpful to the discussion.

Quite clearly therefore, the potential for the largest gain lies in the short term, out-of-the-money options, while the long term, in-the-money options offer the lowest potential for gain.

As far as the degree of risk is concerned, we might be tempted to say that we could use the same +'s to represent the risk for each option, i.e. long term, in-the-money options being the safest, and short term, out-of-the-money being the riskiest. This is much too simple a view. It is sensible to look at risk in terms of being completely wrong about the direction of the share price. If the

Table 7.11. Gains in share prices and option premiums between 4th and 15th December 1987.

Share	Strike Price	4th December 87				15th December 87				Jan Gain	Apr Gain	Jul Gain	Share Gain
		Share Price	Jan Pre	Apr Pre	Jul Pre	Jan Pre	Apr Pre	Jul Pre	Share Price				
Allied Lyons	300	333	37	53	60	60	70	78	352	62.16	32.08	30.00	5.71
	330	333	20	35	42	35	50	60	352	75.00	42.86	42.86	5.71
Brit&Comm	280	295	40	55	75	50	60	75	315	25.00	9.09	0.00	6.78
BP	220	242	32	38	45	30	38	45	237	-6.25	0.00	0.00	20.7
	240	242	16	27	35	15	25	35	237	-6.25	-7.41	0.00	-2.07
Bass	750	778	45	70	93	85	122	145	821	88.89	74.29	55.91	5.53
Cable&Wrlss	280	305	40	50	70	49	63	72	323	22.50	26.00	2.86	5.90
Cons Gold	850	895	100	130	170	110	165	200	910	10.00	26.92	17.65	1.68
Courtaulds	300	317	30	45	60	53	70	78	345	76.67	55.56	30.00	8.83
Comm Union	280	303	34	45	50	83	88	95	357	144.12	95.56	90.00	17.82
	300	303	24	35	40	65	72	82	357	170.83	105.71	105.00	17.82
British Gas	120	122	12	15	22	11	16	21	124	-8.33	6.67	-4.55	1.64
Jaguar	260	263	21	32	42	52	60	73	299	147.62	87.50	73.81	13.69
Marks&Spnc	160	164	15	24	28	26	36	38	181	73.33	50.00	35.71	10.37
Sainsbury	200	212	22	32	38	28	37	44	222	27.27	15.63	15.79	4.72
Storehouse	240	243	25	37	50	30	43	52	263	20.00	16.22	4.00	8.23
Trafalgar Ho	280	295	30	40	52	43	55	65	317	43.33	37.50	25.00	7.4
TSB	100	104	12	15	20	11	16	20	107	8.33	6.67	0.00	2.88
						Average	gain			53.20	37.82	29.11	6.60
							Gearing			8.06	5.73	4.4	

share price falls drastically, then much more capital will be lost with short-term, in-the-money options than any of the others. In these terms therefore it is these that are the riskiest, not their out-of-the-money counterparts. A slightly rosier view of risk may be taken if we look at the position where we are only half right about the movement of the share price, i.e. it neither rises nor falls. In such a case the risk is approximately proportional to the potential gains shown in Table 7.10.

When to buy in-the-money options

Since Table 7.10 shows that the potential for profit with in-the-money options is always less than their out-of-the-money equivalents, it is not surprising that most of the action in traded options takes place in the latter. Although the profit potential of in-the-money options is less, never forget that this potential is very much greater than the potential for profit in the underlying shares

BUYING CALL OPTIONS 103

Table 7.12. Change between 4th and 15th December 1987 for out-of-the-money options

Share	Strike Price	4th December 87							15th December 87				Share Price	Jan Gain	Apr Gain	Jul Gain	Share Gain
		Share Price	Jan Pre	Apr Pre	Jul Pre	Jan Pre	Apr Pre	Jul Pre									
Allied Lyons	360	333	8	22	30	18	35	45					352	125.00	59.09	50.00	5.71
Brit & Comm	300	295	25	50	65	35	45	65					315	40.00	-10.00	0.00	6.78
	330	295	10	30	40	15	30	42					315	50.00	0.00	5.00	6.78
BP	260	242	10	18	26	7	16	25					237	-30.00	-11.11	-3.85	-2.07
Bass	800	778	25	50	72	50	92	118					821	100.00	84.00	63.89	5.53
	850	778	13	32	55	27	65	95					821	107.69	103.13	72.73	5.53
Cable & Wrlss	330	305	12	28	43	17	33	45					323	41.67	17.86	4.65	5.90
Cons Gold	900	895	75	100	140	85	135	175					910	13.33	35.00	25.00	1.68
	950	895	55	80	120	60	105	150					910	9.09	31.25	25.00	1.68
Courtaulds	330	317	13	33	43	30	50	60					345	130.77	51.52	39.53	8.83
	360	317	6	20	32	12	33	45					345	100.00	65.00	40.63	8.83
Comm Union	330	303	10	20	27	38	50	62					357	280.00	150.00	129.63	17.82
	360	303	6	12	22	18	33	47					357	200.00	175.00	113.64	17.82
British Gas	130	122	6	9	16	5	11	15					124	-16.67	22.22	-6.25	1.64
Jaguar	280	263	12	22	34	35	47	60					299	191.67	113.64	76.47	13.69
	300	263	8	19	29	22	36	50					299	175.00	89.47	72.41	13.69
	330	263	5	12	21	11	23	35					299	120.00	91.67	66.67	13.69
Marks&Spncr	180	164	6	15	18	11	22	26					181	83.33	46.67	44.44	10.37
	200	164	2	8	14	4	13	20					181	100.00	62.50	42.86	10.37
Sainsbury	220	212	10	22	28	15	25	33					222	50.00	13.64	17.86	4.72
	240	212	4	14	13	6	17	24					222	50.00	21.43	84.62	4.72
Storehouse	260	243	15	30	40	18	32	40					263	20.00	6.67	0.00	8.23
	280	243	10	23	32	9	22	30					263	-10.00	-4.35	-6.25	8.23
Trafalgar Ho	300	295	20	27	42	28	40	52					317	40.00	48.15	23.81	7.46
	330	295	10	20	30	15	25	37					317	50.00	25.00	23.33	7.46
TSB	110	104	7	11	14	5	10	14					107	-28.57	-9.09	0.00	2.88
	120	104	5	8	11	3	7	10					107	-40.00	-12.50	-9.09	2.88
							Average Gain							72.31	46.88	36.92	6.60
							Average gearing							10.96	7.10	5.59	

themselves. Thus there are attractions in these options for the investor who may be considering buying the shares. The key here is to find options which have been so ignored by other investors that their time values have become too low, offering an extremely good buy. A good example which has already appeared in this Chapter is STC (Table 7.7). Here the time value for the April 220s on 26th February 1988 was down to 2p. Such options - short expiry, reasonably heavily in-the-money approach a delta value of 1 (Chapter 5), i.e. will rise penny for penny with the share price. Thus in the STC case, over the following week the share price rose by 13p, from 243 to 256p, while the option premium rose from 25 to 36p, i.e. 44%. It is usually possible to find one such example every few weeks. The investor employing such a successful strategy now has two courses open to him: he can take his profit in the options, or, if he still requires the shares, he can exercise into them. In the latter event he has in effect partly paid (about 15% of the total in the case of STC) for the shares. Do not forget also the other source of income during this exercise: he could have invested the balance of the sum he had intended to invest in the shares in the money market, easily offsetting the 2p he has had to pay for the time value.

Note that it is in the short term expiry options that opportunities such as that with STC exist. The longer expiry options are unlikely to throw up many situations where the time values are absurdly low.

The level of gains to be made out of the in-the-money options are shown for the period 4th to 15th December 1987 in Table 7.11. Most shares made fairly modest gains over this two weeks. With a few exceptions (Cable and Wireless and Consolidated Goldfields), the short term January options achieved higher gains than the medium or longer expiry options. The average gain in the January options was 53.2%, the April options 37.8% and the July options 29.1%. The share prices averages a gain of 6.6%. Thus the gearing given by the January options was an average factor of 8, fully justifying the case for investment in the short term, in-the-money options at a time when modest gains are expected in the share price. Change between 4th and 15th December 1987

Out-of-the-money options

As was stated earlier, most of the action in the traded options market occurs in the out-of-the-money options. In these options the length of time to expiry becomes of paramount importance. Before looking in more detail at these options, some general observations are in order:

1. Volatility is of prime importance. A share of low volatility will rise so slowly that short expiry options may see little movement in the time remaining to expiry. Do not consider far out-of-the-money options unless the share is in the top half of the volatility league table.

BUYING CALL OPTIONS   105

```
GAIN IN
OPTION
VALUE
```
(graph showing gain in option value rising then flattening as share price increases)

SHARE PRICE

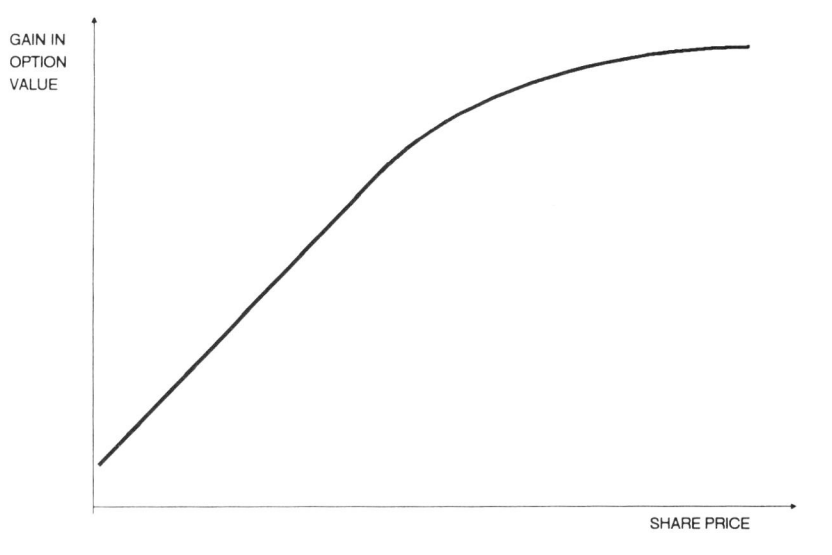

Figure 7.4. Fall off in the gain of an option with time even though share price continues upwards at a constant rate.

2. Base your decision as to whether to invest in short, medium or long expiry times on the result of channel analysis on the underlying share. This should give you a firm idea of the length of time for which the coming share price rise will endure. Expiry dates should be chosen so as to coincide as near as is possible to this period of rise in order to maximise the gearing obtained.

It is interesting to compare the gains made in the out-of-the-money versions of the options which were shown in Table 7.11. These values are given in Table 7.12. Taken as an average, the gains made are approximately twice as much as those made in the in-the-money options, illustrating the extra gearing to be obtained from the out-of-the-money options.

Tired Options

Note that as the share price continues to rise, the gains being made on a week by week basis in a particular option, especially one with the nearest expiry, will start to fall off. This is shown in Figure 7.4 for the theoretical case where the share price continues upwards at a constant rate. It can be seen that the gain in the option starts to flatten out as time goes on. There are several reasons for this. As discussed earlier, the time values of the options start to erode over the last six weeks or so of the life of the option, putting the brake on the upward movement in the premium. A further factor is that the longer the upward movement in the share price continues, the more does the traded options market consider that it is coming to an end, so that the demand for that particular option declines. This naturally has an adverse effect on the option premium. The logic of this situation is that, if we neglect the impact of the buying and selling costs, there comes a point at which we should close the position and open a different one, even though the share price is still rising. As shown in the next section, if we feel that the share price rise still has some steam left in it, it is sensible to close the current position and open another one in a different option of that share.

SUBSEQUENT ACTION

Once an option has been bought, then the position must be constantly monitored to see that the expected upward share price trend is maintained within the timescale of the option expiry date. Two outcomes require that action is taken other than that intended when the option was purchased. The first is a fall in the share price, and the second is when the upward trend in the share price appears to be exceeding the original expectation and you wish to profit further from the extended movement.

Falling Share Price

Action here depends upon whether you feel the price will continue to fall or whether it will rally from what you consider is a temporary situation. In the former case the best thing is to close the position. In the latter case you could sweat it out by doing nothing and waiting for the share price recovery to improve the value of your option. A much better strategy which will reduce the risk in your position is to roll down.

Rolling Down

This strategy will reduce the risk in your position at the cost of reducing the potential profit. There are two legs to this strategy, which will end up with you holding a bull spread (see Chapter 11). A bull spread is one where you write a call with one striking price and buy a call with a lower striking price, and since the share price is falling, obviously we will have to buy another call with a lower striking price than the present one. In order to convert our holding of the higher strike price call into a written position on that option, we will have to write two contracts on the option series that we originally held. Thus:

1. Write two contracts for the same option that we held originally.

2. Buy one contract in an option with a lower striking price.

All of these transaction should be carried out on options of the same expiry date as the original, provided of course that there is sufficient time left to expiry. If the latter is the case, then move out into further expiring options if you are convinced that the amended timescale you see for the upward turn to the current downtrend is appropriate.

Rising Share price

If the upward trend is as you expected, then maintain the present position in the option or close it if you have achieved your objective. If you are convinced that the price rise will be prolonged, then the appropriate strategy is to roll up. *Note that you should only undertake this action if you are convinced that the opportunity for profit by staying with this share is greater or more imminent than opportunities with other shares which may just be entering a new upward phase.*

Rolling Up the Options

This is the strategy to employ where you feel that a share price movement, which has given you a useful profit in your selected call option, may continue for some considerable time, possibly past the expiry date of your option. In such a case therefore you need to continue your involvement with options in that share. However, you will be putting at risk profits that you have already made from the current option that you hold, and therefore you must be convinced that the upward price trend will continue for some time.

The strategy involves the following actions:

1. Closing your current position in the option.

2. Buying an option with a higher striking price.

The strategy takes into account the comments made in the last section about tired options. Since the most gearing will be obtained with the shorter expiry options, the investor should stick with these, with the proviso that they should only be bought if they have more than about six weeks left to expiry. This is because, as we have stated previously, time values start to decay rapidly over this final period. Because of this, the amount of gearing available from the option starts to fall off compared with that from options with a further out expiry date. We also pointed out (Table 7.8) that as the option moves into the at-the-money or in-the-money position due to the share price rise, the fall off in time values becomes more marked. Thus, as a general rule, we can say that it is time to move out of the option once the share price has more or less reached the striking price. This gives us an automatic selling signal for the option. The new option should be the most out-of-the money option, which will of course have been newly introduced as a result of the share price rise (see Chapter 2).

Thus our strategy becomes:-

1. Sell once the share price reaches the striking price, or if the option was initially in-the-money, sell when there are only a few weeks left to expiry.

2. Buy the most out-of-the-money option with the nearest expiry date that has at least six weeks to run.

Date	Share price	Transaction			Amount £
20/02/88	207	Buy 10 contracts	May 240s @	6p	600
04/03/88	237	Sell 10 contracts	May 240s @	14p	1400
		Buy 20 contracts	May 260s @	7p	1400
30/04/88	316	Sell 20 contracts	May 260s @	60p	12000
		Buy 40 contracts	Aug 330s @	30p	12000
25/06/88	347	Sell 40 contracts	Aug 330s @	50p	20000

Percentage gain = 3233%   WR = 3233 x 52/18 = 9339%

This policy will bring to bear the maximum gearing, and hence the maximum profit during the course of the share price rise. The number of contracts being bought will escalate dramatically. A close watch has to be kept on the share price using all available techniques, especially channel analysis, in order to determine the point at which the strategy should be terminated. This is essential, since at the end of a successful series of these transactions, an enormous sum of money will be at risk relative to the initial starting sum. This is well illustrated by an example based on the rise in the Racal share price from 207p to 347p over the four month period from February to June 1988.

The gain of 67.6% in the share price was transformed by the gearing of options into a gain of 3233% by using this strategy over just three complete buying and selling operations. This resulted in just £600 being converted into £20,000! Note that the price rise just before 30th April was so rapid that the principle of selling once the share price equalled the striking price was overtaken by events. Note also that £12,000 was riding on the last buying transaction, emphasizing the necessity for the utmost vigilance during this last phase of the Racal share price rise.

CHAPTER 8

Writing Call Options

The writer of a call option receives a premium from a buyer of the option and in return undertakes to sell the shares at the striking price if a buyer exercises the option.

Much time was spent in the last Chapter on a discussion of the relationship between share prices and option premiums, including a careful consideration of time values. These relationships are also of course of paramount importance to the seller, i.e. the writer of a call option, but since the topic has been covered in detail, it will not be repeated here. The writer of a call option is naturally at the opposite side of the transaction to the purchaser, and therefore on a simple view he takes a diametrically opposed position about the future movement of the share price.

While the purchaser expects a rise in the share price during the lifetime of the option, and can buy an option which will reflect his view of the extent of the rise and the timescale over which it will occur, the writer expects either a fall in the share price, a static share price, or a rise so limited that it would not be profitable for the buyer to exercise the option. This reference to exercising the option draws attention to a major important difference which a newcomer to the purchase of call options can overlook: the buyer of the option has control of the situation while the writer does not. The buyer can exercise the option at any time during its lifetime, in which case the writer has to provide the requisite number of shares in the underlying security, usually 1000 shares per option contract (see Chapter 2).

There are then two positions in which the writer can find himself - he already owns the shares and can deliver, or he will have to buy the shares in the market in order to deliver. The first type of investor is called a 'covered' writer, and the second category an 'uncovered' or 'naked' writer.

As the discussion proceeds, it will become apparent that the naked writer is exposed to a very high level of risk, while the covered writer can be considered to be quite a conservative investor.

NAKED OPTION WRITING

The opposed positions of a purchaser of a call option and the writer of the call option are most obviously illustrated by the naked option writer. In the last Chapter we defined the option purchaser's position as being one of limited loss and unlimited gain. The naked writer is in the unfortunate position of having a position of unlimited loss and limited gain. The gain is limited because it is simply the premium, less expenses, obtained by selling the option. The loss is unlimited because the writer has to buy the shares in the market if the option is exercised. In theory he may have to pay an infinitely high price for them.

Loss/gain potential - unlimited loss, limited gain

Just as in the last Chapter, we can draw a diagram to illustrate this concept of limited gain and unlimited loss for the naked option writer by plotting the profit or loss potential against the share price. This is shown in Figure 8.1.

At the point A, the share price is equal to the striking price and the purchaser would be considering exercising the option. The profit, i.e. the original premium) has remained constant up to this point, but as the share price moves above the striking price, the writer has to pay an increasing amount to buy the shares in order to deliver them when the option is exercised. At the point B, the original premium received has been wiped out. Since the share price has in theory no upper limit, then the loss incurred will also have no limit.

Because of this relationship between profit and loss for naked option writing, it is not to be recommended to the novice in the traded options market.

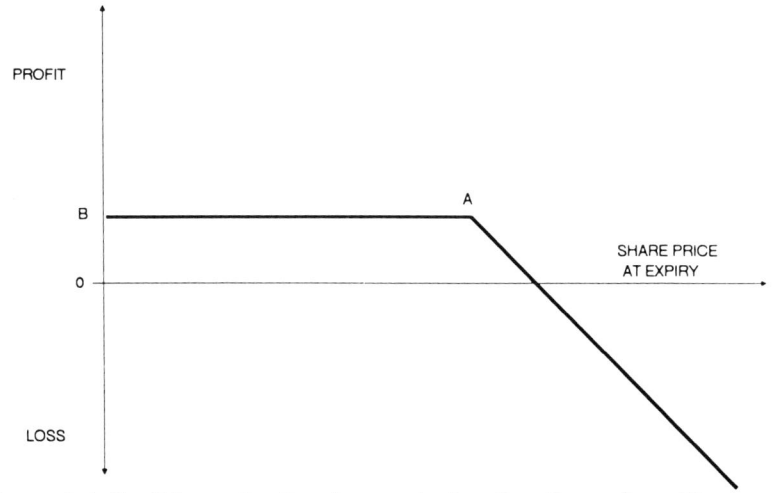

Figure 8.1. Profit/loss situation for a naked call option writer with changing share price. The point A is the striking price and the point B is the premium received.

Financial disaster can be the outcome of an incorrect decision about the future share price movement. The writer must be extremely confident of a fall in the price of the underlying security. Although of course the written position can be cancelled simply by the purchase of an identical number of contracts in the same option, this cannot be done, under the rules of the traded options market, once the writer has received an exercise notice. The writer is therefore vulnerable to the sort of sharp upward price movements that occur upon the news of a takeover bid. In such situations the writer may simply not have the time to take corrective action by closing the position. The naked option writer should always adopt the policy of closing his position at the first hint that matters are going against him, rather than wait in the hope that the situation will change.

Margin Requirements for Writing Call Options

An option writer must deposit cover with the London Options Clearing House by 10 a.m. the business day following the day of the bargain. This can be arranged via the broker. The cover can be in several forms, such as a bank confirmation that it holds the share certificates, or convertible issues, bearer bonds, etc, of the company in whose shares the option is being written, to the order of the London Option Clearing House. In the case of a naked writer, he must deposit a margin of 25% of the value of the underlying security, adjusted by the extent to which the option series stands in- or out-of-the-money. The sum deposited by the naked option writer has to be adjusted on a daily basis as the share price moves. As the share price moves upwards, the required margin increases, and decreases as the share price falls.

Exercise of Call Options

Much of the discussion so far has had to consider the position when the option is exercised against the writer, since this is the point at which the upside potential becomes realised. From the point of view of the writer therefore, the exercise of the option is not a good outcome of the investment position. Simplistically, it might be thought that an option would be exercised once it moves sufficiently in-the-money to more than cover the premium paid and any expenses involved in the purchase of the option and the purchase of the shares. That this does not happen is due to the fact that, early in the life of an option, the purchaser is generally not looking towards the purchase of the shares as the means to generating a profit, but to the selling of the option at a much higher value than he has paid for it. Thus, early in the life of options, only a very small proportion are exercised, while the majority, if they do not expire worthless are exercised in the last few weeks prior to expiry.

As we have pointed out, however, the writer is completely at the mercy of the purchaser, and should not take for granted that the option will not be exercised against him, however much time is left until expiry. Note that the purchaser and writer of the corresponding option are matched against each other in a random selection by computer as being the fairest way to do this.

COVERED OPTION WRITING

While the writing of uncovered options is an extremely aggressive investment stance, the writing of covered options is extremely conservative, and is frequently less risky than simply buying shares themselves. The writing of a covered option can be used in the sense of an insurance against a fall in share price, thereby reducing the downside exposure. It can be used also as a means of improving the overall return on an investment. The improvements in the potential for loss obviously have to paid for, and this payment is the loss of the potential for gain beyond a certain point (the striking price), since a rise in the share price can result in the option being exercised and the consequent loss of the shareholding.

Compared with simply holding the shares, covered option writing is superior when:

1. The share price falls
2. The share price remains static
3. The share price enjoys a small rise

In the latter case, the extent to which the written option is in-the-money or out-of-the-money is of vital importance. The further the option is out-of-the-money, the greater is the tolerance to small share price rises.

Loss/Gain Potential - Limited Loss, Limited Gain

This fundamental property of covered option writing can be illustrated by a diagram similar to that used for naked options, by plotting the potential profit or loss against the share price.

Ignoring dealing costs, the maximum loss which can be incurred is the cost of the shares less the premium received for writing the options, and of course this loss will only occur if the value of the shares fall to zero. The point A, where the share price is above the sum of the striking price plus the premium which the purchaser has paid for the option, we can assume is the lowest share price at which the option will be exercised. The maximum profit is therefore obtainable at point A, and will not change as the share price rises further above this point. The profit is equal to the premium obtained plus the difference

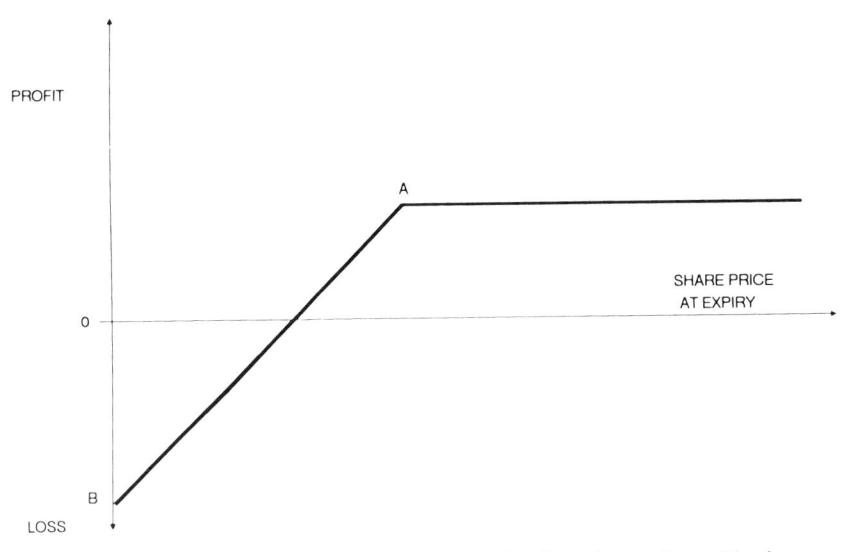

Figure 8.2. Profit/loss situation for a covered call option writer with changing share price. The point A is the striking price and the point B is equal to the striking price - share price + the premium received.

between the striking price (the price at which the writer has to deliver the shares to the purchaser) and the share price which was paid when the shares were bought. Quite clearly, this difference may be positive or negative, depending upon whether the option is out-, at-, or in-the-money. Bearing in mind that option premiums get lower as we proceed from in-the-money to out-of-the-money, we can make the following generalisations, since the profit can be described by the relationship:

PROFIT = PREMIUM (A) + STRIKING PRICE (B)
 - PRICE ORIGINALLY PAID FOR SHARES (C)

Type of option	A	B - C
In-the-money	* * *	negative
At-the-money	* *	zero
Out-of-the-money	*	positive

Thus the higher premium for the in-the-money option is offset by the fact that when the shares are called, the investor receives less than he has paid for them. At the other extreme, the lower premium for out-of-the-money options will have an additional amount added, thereby improving the profit. Since the pricing of options is not an exact science, we would not expect the net result of adding A to (B - C) to be the same for all types of options. This fact is best illustrated by an actual example based on the data presented for the Courtaulds option in the last Chapter. On 4th March 1988, the data for Courtaulds was as follows:

Share price 331p April 300s, 36p; 330s, 18p; 360s, 7p July 300s, 48p; 330s, 30p; 360s, 17p October 300s, 55p; 330s, 36p; 360s, 25p

We will assume that the investor buys the shares at this price of 331p. For our purposes, the 330 options can be considered to be at-the-money, since the share price was 331p.

Taking just the April options, the profit made from the options at expiry are shown in Table 8.1

We can take the 'If exercised' column to have a different meaning, i.e. the

Table 8.1. Profit made from Courtaulds April options, share price 331p

Type of option		If exercised	If not exercised
In-the-money	300s	36 + 300 - 331 = 5	36
At-the-money	330s	18 + 330 - 331 = 17	18
Out-of-the-money	360s	7 + 360 - 331 = 36	7

'upside potential', since the option will be exercised if the share price rises. Conversely the 'If not exercised' column means the 'downside protection' since the option will not be exercised if the share price falls. On this basis therefore we can see that the following is true:

In-the-money call options writing: high protection on the downside
low potential on the upside

At-the-money call options writing: moderate protection on the downside
moderate potential on the upside

Out-of-the-money call options writing: low protection on the downside
high potential on the upside

Thus, before considering in more detail which particular option should be written, it is important for the option writer to define his objectives in terms of profit potential and downside protection. Naturally, the more conservative investor would opt for the downside protection, and therefore would tend to write in-the-money options.

Timescale

As was the case with the purchase of call options, the prime consideration with option writing is to obtain a view of the timescale of the trend that you are taking advantage of, preferable by means of channel analysis. Since a prime consideration is to avoid having your shares called away, the expiry date of the option being written should be nearer than the anticipated length of time for which the trend will continue. It is best to take an opposite view of time from that taken by the purchaser of the option. Purchasers will tend to take the view that it might be worth paying the higher premiums for longer expiry options because there is more time for an adverse trend to reverse direction and put the option into profit. As far as the writer of an call option is concerned, he has already pocketed the premium, and therefore the sooner the option expires the better, since there is less chance of the option being exercised. Of course, this comes down to a straight trade-off between extra premium that can be obtained for writing longer expiry options and the additional risk that the option will be exercised.

A further point here is to consider the return from the investment as a weekly return (WR). If the premiums for the 9 month, 6 month and 3 month options were in the ratio of 3 to 2 to 1 in cost, then of course the WRs would be the same. The relationship between short, medium and long term expiry premiums can be examined by extracting some data from Table 7.1 from the last Chapter. The data is shown in Table 8.2, where the premiums have been divided by the number of months to expiry, thus giving a value for the premium to be paid/received per month to expiry.

Quite obviously with a particular option class, the further out the expiry date, the less is the premium per month remaining. This is fine for the purchasers of the option, since they are reducing their costs per month by going for the longer term. As far as the writer of an option is concerned, he is receiving less premium per month for the longer expiry options, i.e. his WR is less.

With these constraints, more attention can be given to option premiums and time values with a view to moving the odds in the favourable direction for the option writer. Two major areas for consideration here will be those options with anomalous time values, and options with high CPPs.

Anomalous Time Values

The purchaser of a call option can frequently spot an anomalous situation where the time value is ludicrously small for the amount of time remaining to expiry. In the last Chapter we drew attention to the STC April 220s, where the

116 TRADED OPTIONS SIMPLIFIED

Table 8.2. Premiums per month remaining to expiry for the options listed in Table 7.1. The data is for 26th February 1988 and share pricdes are given in parentheses.

Option		Expiry Month	Prem. P/Mth	Expiry Month	Prem. P/Mth	Expiry Month	Prem. P/Mth
Dixons	180	March	12.0	June	5.5	September	3.9 (187p)
	200		3.0		3.0		2.4
	220		1.5		1.5		1.7
Trafalgar	300	April	19.0	July	9.0	October	6.5 (329)
	330		9.0		5.4		4.4
	360		3.5		2.8		3.1
Brit. Tele	220	May	10.0	August	6.0	November	4.6 (244)
	240		5.3		3.5		3.2
	260		2.1		2.0		1.9

time value was down to 2p as early as 26th February, i.e. with nearly eight weeks remaining to expiry. The exact opposite view has to be taken by the writer of the option - he is looking for situations where the time value appears too high for the circumstances, i.e. for the amount of time remaining to expiry. This means he will receive a higher premium than normal for a certain risk. It should be borne in mind that time values are at their highest for options which are at-the-money, or at least very close to that position.

Probably the most fruitful area, since it will be more easily spotted and understood, will be the short expiry options, which of course we have already indicated are the most sensible for the option writer in any case. Options where the time values are high for the amount of time remaining to expiry should stand out from the rest. Of course the main reason for high time values is an upward surge in the share price, so we have to ignore those options where the underlying share price has been particularly buoyant. We have to look for options where the share price has remained static or has fallen, but where the time values are too optimistic for the situation.

There are sometimes situations where although the share price has risen over a one or two week period, channel analysis or moving average analysis is showing that a peak is about to be reached and the share price will then start to move downwards. To rush in and write such an option under such circumstances is to take an unnecessary risk. It is vital if channel analysis shows that a peak or trough is about to be reached that the investor waits until the peak or trough has just been passed, i.e. that the prediction has been confirmed, since the investor should be trying to get into his investment position at the beginning of a trend. Failure to do this and instead try to anticipate peaks and

WRITING CALL OPTIONS 117

Hawker Siddeley up to 22nd April 1988

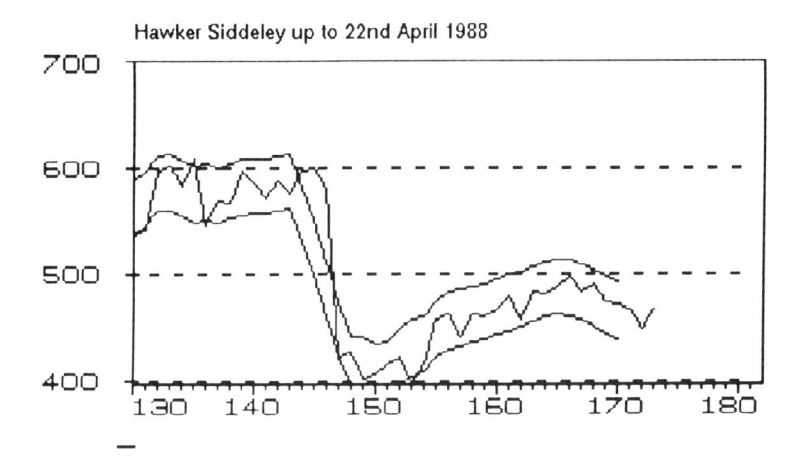

Figure 8.3. Hawker Siddeley share price up to 22nd April 1988.

troughs will inevitably lead to failure, since there are many occasions where a channel will develop an adverse hook to its previous direction. Besides the reduction in risk that will accompany this way of approaching the investment, there is a more direct value to the option writer - the rise in share price to its peak value will carry the option premium with it, and therefore the profit potential in writing that particular option will have increased.

This point can be well illustrated by taking Hawker Siddeley as an example. In Figure 8.3 is shown the share price chart up to 22nd April 1988. The price of 470p on 22nd April is considerably higher than the low point of 451p reached the week before, and is suggesting that 451p represented an intermediate trough. Since the top boundary of the channel is obviously well defined by a number of points since the beginning of 1988, this 451p level does match the most sensible lower boundary which can be drawn so as to be at a constant distance below the well defined upper one. Note the very important fact that the longer term trend of Hawker Siddeley is upwards! Because of this it would be totally wrong to write options other than the shortest expiry. If we ignored channel analysis for even the short term prediction and just decided that 22nd April was a good time to write an option because we just think that the overall trend of the share price is downwards, the positions would be:

Share price 470p, June 420s, 57p; June 460s, 25p; June 500s, 9p

118 TRADED OPTIONS SIMPLIFIED

Option	If exercised (upside potential)	If not exercised (downside protection)	U/D ratio
June 420s	(57 + 420 - 470) = 7	57	0.122
460s	(25 + 460 - 470) = 15	25	0.6
500s	(9 + 500 - 470) = 39	9	4.33

The U/D ratio of 4.33 for the June 500s represents a good opportunity for the less conservative investor.

Using channel analysis, the upper boundary in Figure 8.3(a), projected forward a few weeks into the future, would suggest that somewhere around the 520p mark would represent the next intermediate peak. The share price reached 523p on 20th May. A few days later the price had dropped to 515p, confirming that 523p was the peak price for the present. By 27th May, the positions were:

Share price 505p, June 420s, 90p; June 460s, 50p; June 500s, 22p

These options give the following figures for upside potential and downside protection:

Option	If exercised (upside potential)	If not exercised (downside protection)	U/D ratio
June 420s	(90 + 420 - 505) = 15	90	0.167
460s	(50 + 460 - 505) = 15	50	0.3
500s	(22 + 500 - 505) = 17	22	0.77

These are obviously far superior to the premiums which would have been obtained a month earlier, and the investor would have the added advantage that only a few weeks were left to expiry. It turned out that the share price was little changed at expiry of the June options.

The above example illustrates quite clearly the increase in the downside protection that is obtained when timing of the investment is improved by means of channel analysis.

The above strategy was one of waiting for the correct opportunity to write an option in a particular share. Naturally, some investors are impatient, and do not relish having to wait before they can take action. If you happen to be the impatient type of investor who has to get involved immediately then the

Table 8.4. Premiums and share prices for September options on 24th June and 8th July 1988.

Share	Series	24th June 1988		8th July 1988	
		Premium	Share Price	Premium	Share Price
Amstrad	Sep 220s	11	206	12	213
Beecham	Sep 500s	12	465	11	472
BTR	Sep 280s	12	274	17	285
Blue Circle	Sep 460s	10	424	32	467
Dixons	Sep 200s	5.5	183	2	177
Glaxo	Sep1000s	50	972	48	985
Hawker	Sep 550s	18	510	18	518
Hillsdown	Sep 300s	11	285	7	283
Hanson	Sep 160s	2.25	143	2.25	145
Lonrho	Sep 260s	8.5	247	11	259
Midland	Sep 460s	15	439	14	445
Sears	Sep 130s	4.5	118	5.5	123
Tesco	Sep 160s	8	156	5	149
Thorn-EMI	Sep 650s	22	649	23	638
Unilever	Sep 500s	18	478	17	478
Wellcome	Sep 550s	33	535	27	532

simplest answer is to look for another option which is not giving conflicting signals. After all, there are plenty to choose from.

Returning to the simple approach of anomalous time values, we can take, as an example the premiums of the out-of-the-money options (and therefore the premiums will equal the time value) on 24th June 1988 and 8th July 1988. For the short expiry September options, these are shown in Table 8.4.

The five shares which fell or remained static over the two week period were: Dixons, Hillsdown, Tesco, Thorn-EMI, Unilever and Wellcome. The premiums/time values for these on 8th July were: 2, 7, 23, 17 and 27p respectively. For our purposes, not only are we looking at the size of the premium, but also at the degree to which the option is standing out-of-the-money, since as we have seen earlier, we have a greater upside potential the further out-of-the-money the option is. Ignoring the first two on the grounds that the premiums are really two low to be of interest, we have to look more closely at Thorn-EMI, Unilever and Wellcome.

120 TRADED OPTIONS SIMPLIFIED

Table 8.5. Cost per percentage point (CPP) values for various options on 8th July 1988.

Share	Series	Premium	Share Price	CPP	Share price at expiry
Amstrad	Sep 220s	12	213	1.35	200
Beecham	Sep 500s	11	472	1.33	459
BTR	Sep 280s	17	285	4.04	285
Blue Circle	Sep 460s	32	467	5.98	437
Dixons	Sep 200s	2	177	0.14	154
Glaxo	Sep 1000s	48	985	7.50	1047
Hawker	Sep 550s	18	518	1.86	513
Hillsdown	Sep 300s	7	283	0.83	262
Hanson	Sep 160s	2.25	145	0.19	143
Lonrho	Sep 260s	11	259	2.37	338
Midland	Sep 460s	14	445	2.15	421
Sears	Sep 130s	5.5	123	0.54	134
Tesco	Sep 160s	5	149	0.47	134
Thorn-EMI	Sep 650s	23	638	4.19	628
Unilever	Sep 500s	17	478	2.08	462
Wellcome	Sep 550s	27	532	3.19	488

The Thorn-EMI Sep 650s were about 2% out-of-the-money, the Unilever Sep 500s about 5% out-of-the-money, and the Wellcome Sep 550s about 3.5% out-of-the-money. On this basis the Unilever and Wellcome options offer by far the best writing opportunity. Neither of these options moved into an in-the-money position up to expiry time and so resulted in useful profits. It must be reiterated that the investor should not write options simply on the basis of two weeks' data such as that given above, but should have come to a view about the near term direction of the share price. The above Table has to be used in the sense of confirming the direction of the price movement as being downwards over a short period such as two weeks, and then making the best selection of the option to be written.

At the time of writing of these options on 8th July, the upside potential and downside protections for both Unilever and Wellcome were:

WRITING CALL OPTIONS

Unilever:
Upside potential = 17 + 500 - 478 = 39p
Downside protection = 17p
Therefore U/D ratio = 2.29

Wellcome:
Upside potential = 27 + 550 - 532 = 45p
Downside protection = 27p
Therefore U/D ratio = 1.67

On these figures Wellcome offer an advantage to the less bullish investor in giving a relatively better downside protection. For the more bullish investor Unilever offers a higher profit potential but at the expense of less downside protection.

Cost Per Percentage Point (CPP)

The method of calculating CPPs was discussed in Chapter 5. It was shown that options with low CPPs were advantageous for the buyer. Conversely therefore, options with high CPPs are going to be advantageous to the writer of options. The CPPs for the same options as were listed in Table 8.4 are given in Table 8.5. Since there are 16 options entered in the Table, we can select the top eight, and these are: Glaxo, Blue Circle, Thorn-EMI, BTR, Wellcome, Lonrho, Midland and Hawker.

Of these top eight, all were on a rising trend except for Thorn-EMI and Wellcome. If channel analysis is not applied, then logic would dictate that either of these two should be the selected vehicle for writing. The upside potential and downside protection has already been calculated for Wellcome. The Thorn-EMI position is:

Upside potential = 23 + 650 - 638 = 35p
Downside protection = 23p
Therefore U/D ratio = 1.52

Since the premium for Wellcome (45p) is larger, then Wellcome is the obvious option to go for.

The last column in the Table shows the share prices at expiry of the September options. Only Glaxo, Lonrho and Sears showed a rise in share price between 8th July and the September expiry. It is interesting to look at the Glaxo case further, since the CPP value for Glaxo was the highest in Table 8.4. The upside potential and downside protection for Glaxo is:

Upside potential = 48 + 1000 - 985 = 63p

Downside protection = 48p
Therefore U/D ratio = 1.31

The temptation to go for Glaxo on the basis of these figures is quite high, since there is high profit potential and high loss protection. Since the share price enjoyed a 6% rise in the period to the expiry of the September options, it is essential to see if this rise could have been foreseen. The chart of the Glaxo share price to the relevant date, 8th July 1988 is shown in Figure 8.4.

The chart shows that since the market crash in October 1987, the Glaxo price has seen one peak and one trough. Since the crash established a drastic hook in the existing channel, the new direction of the channel can only be defined by at least two peaks and a trough, or two troughs and a peak. We are therefore in a situation where the channel is not defined, unlike the case for Hawker Siddeley in Figure 8.3 where the channel was very clearly defined. In such a case as Glaxo, it is not possible to take a sensible view of the course of the share price in the near future, and therefore the writing or buying of such options is to be avoided.

SUBSEQUENT ACTION

We have already stated that the covered call out-performs a straightforward purchase of the shares if the share price subsequently falls, stays static or rises slightly. Our constant theme as traded options investors must be to monitor the position constantly and react rapidly if the share price starts to behave differently from your initial projection. The two extreme trends which will require a reaction other than to leave things as they are are firstly a rapid fall in share price and secondly a rise in share price that looks as if it could be the start of a longer uptrend.

Rapid Fall in Share Price

Although a covered call gives you a measure of downside protection in the form of the additional premium that you have received, this is worth most to the investor when the share price fall is modest. Anything more than that will mean a considerable fall in the value of the investment. The best action in this situation is the same that you would take if you simply held the shares themselves: sell when selling signals such as moving averages tell you to (see Stocks and Shares Simplified). By virtue of the premium that you have received, you still come out ahead of the investor who did not write options against his shareholding.

WRITING CALL OPTIONS 123

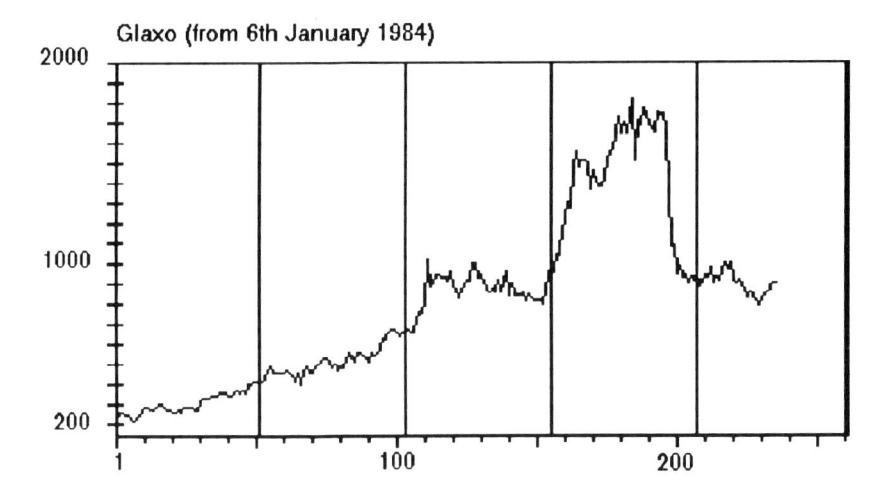

Figure 8.4. Glaxo share price to 8th July 1988.

Prolonged Rise in Share Price

If the share price rises above the striking price, then you become increasingly at risk to the option being called and thus losing the underlying shares, albeit at a higher price than you paid for them. You will of course receive the return that would have been calculated as the upside potential when the position was first taken. As an alternative to this, it is possible to carry out a rolling up procedure that can increase the return significantly above that from the initial position.

Rolling Up

The procedure and effect on the profit/loss potentials is best illustrated by using and example such as STC. On 12th February 1988 the share price was 221p and the out-of-the-money April 240 calls were 9p. An investor buying the shares and selling the call at these prices would have bought the shares at a net cost of 221 - 9 = 212p. By 26th February the share price had risen to 243p and the April 240s to 16p. The premium for the April 260s was 8p. If the investor was becoming convinced that the share price would continue to rise but decided to take no action, he would eventually see the call exercised against him. In such a situation, his profit would the exercise price less the net price he paid for the shares, i.e. 240 - 212 = 28p.

The percentage profit = 28 x 100/212 = 13.2%.

Instead of doing nothing, the investor could have rolled up the option. This means closing the April 240 written call by purchasing an April 240 call, now at 16p and writing an April 260 call, i.e. further out-of-the-money, at 8p. The net cost of the shares is now 221 - 9 + 16 - 8 = 220p. He has now of course had to invest 9p more in the position than his original investment. In return, if the share price continues to rise and the option is exercised, he will receive 260p for the shares, giving a profit of 40p.

This is equal to a percentage profit of 40 x 100/220 = 18.2%.

The net effect of rolling up the position once the investor became convinced that the share price would continue to rise was that the investor was able to participate in this rise to a level of 260p rather than 240p, which was the original striking price. This improved the profit from 13% to 18%, neglecting dealing costs.

This example serves to illustrate, if such is needed, the flexibility of traded options as an investment vehicle. Even when the original prediction of the investor begins to turn sour, there is still plenty of scope to change the position to take advantage of the changed circumstances.

CHAPTER 9

Buying Put Options

A put option gives the purchaser of the option the right to sell a number, usually 1000, shares in the underlying security at a fixed price - the striking price - at any time up to the expiry of the option. As shown in Chapter 6, buying puts is the strategy for those investors who have bearish expectations for the share price. The buyer expects that the value of the option, expressed in terms of its premium, will increase as the share price falls, and just like the buyer of a call option, he expects a high level of gearing (in this case a reverse gearing), i.e. the gain in the value of the option is much greater than the fall in the share price. The strategy is attended by a moderate amount of risk, limited to the amount of the premium that has been paid. The holder of a put option has a large, though limited, potential for gain. The gain is limited by the fact that the share price has an ultimate lower value of just above zero, perhaps 0.5 or 1p. A value of zero would of course imply that the company has ceased trading and the shares therefore have no value. In such a case there would be no dealings, and therefore the right that the option gives to sell the shares at the striking price would no longer apply.

As with call options, a major attraction of put options for the investor with bearish expectations for the share price is that there is a large variety of options available, so that the investor can tailor his investment to the amount of risk he is prepared to accept. As with other options, the potential for profit in a put option is proportional to the amount of risk which is accepted, although there are many instances where options have anomalous premiums which are lower than expected for the particular circumstances. These can provide much lower risk situations for the alert investor.

Loss-Gain Potential - Limited Loss, Large, though Limited Gain

The profit or loss potential of a put option can be plotted as a function of the share price at expiry to give a graph of characteristic shape as shown in Figure 9.1. The point A on the horizontal axis represents the striking price. As the share price at expiry falls below this point, the profit increases as an upward sloping line, being limited only by the lowest possible tradeable share price of just above zero. In the opposite direction, as the share price rises the profit

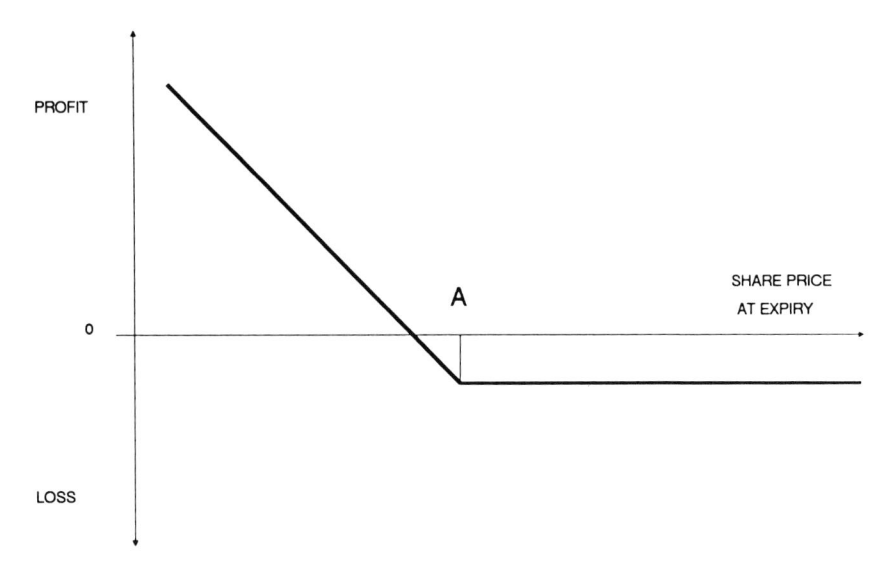

Figure 9.1. Gain or loss for a put option.

decreases until the value of the option is the same as the original premium paid. A further rise in share price to the point A, at which it is equal to the striking price, reduces the value to zero, hence the maximum loss at that point is the original premium paid.

The graph illustrates a major attribute of a put option - the loss is limited while the gain is, although also limited, many many times larger.

Option Premiums

In order to provide a comparison with call options, we can take the premiums for put options in the same underlying shares, and at the same time, 26th February 1988 as Table 7.1 in Chapter 7.

Bearing in mind the opposite nature of in-the-money, etc. for put options compared with call options, i,.e. the higher striking prices are in-the-money for puts whereas the lower striking prices are in-the-money for calls, there are two points which are general in application and which can be seen from Table 9.1:

1. The least expensive option is always the nearer expiry, furthest out-of-the-money option, e.g. Dixons March 180s, Trafalgar House April 300s and the British Telecom May 220s.

Table 9.1. Premiums for various put options on 26th February 1988.

Share	Price	Option	Expiry Date and Premium		
Dixons	187	180	[MAR] 4	[JUN]	10[SEP]
		200	16	23	26
		220	34	34	40
Trafalgar House	329	300	[APR]7	[JUL]12	[OCT]15
		330	17	25	28
		360	37	43	48
British Telecom	244	220	[MAY]3.5	[AUG]8	[NOV]12
		240	9.5	16	18
		260	19	26	30

2. *The most expensive option is always the furthest expiry, deepest in-the-money options, i.e. Dixons September 220s, Trafalgar House October 360s and British Telecom November 260s.*

Any table of option prices in a newspaper will confirm these two facts. The nearer expiry, furthest out-of-the-money options are cheaper because they have no intrinsic value (being out-of-the-money) and their time values will be lower than the longer expiry options because of the lack of time in which they can move into a profitable position before the expiry date by virtue of a fall in share price. The corollary of this is that the deepest in-the-money options have an intrinsic value and the further expiry options higher time values because there is plenty of time available during which the share price can fall, this improving the value of the premium.

As we commented for call options, we can go no further than these two simple statements in trying to generalise from one class of options to another. The premium for the March 200 puts for one share is unlikely to be the same as the premium for the March 200 puts for another share. We can however look more closely at the premiums within an option class by looking at their time values and intrinsic values. This sort of analysis will help in selecting the best option for a particular set of investment circumstances.

Relationship Between Premiums and Share Price

Before investing in any type of option, the investor will obviously have come to a conclusion about the direction of the share price and the time for which this direction will be maintained. He may have come to the conclusion by using the principles already discussed in this book, or he may have other ways of analysing share prices. Attention will now focus on a correct choice of option, and a knowledge of how put option prices may be expected to move as the underlying share price moves will be of paramount importance. This movement will be magnified in the case of options which are of short expiry date, and therefore these offer the most fruitful area to study. As in the case of call options, there are three scenarios:

1. The share price will remain static - the RISK

2. A downward share price movement occurs - the REWARD

3. The share price rises - the RISK

Since all premiums are composed of an intrinsic value (which might be zero) and a time value, the effect on intrinsic values and time values for each of the three share price movements listed above can be discussed.

Intrinsic Values

The intrinsic value for a put option is the difference between the striking price and the share price where this difference is positive, i.e. where the share can be put at a higher price than the actual share price. Because of this mathematical fact, the following observations will be true:

1. Static price movement will leave intrinsic values unchanged.

2. Downward share price movement will increase intrinsic values on a penny for penny basis, and some options with zero intrinsic value will move into a state of positive intrinsic value as the movement continues.

3. Upward price movement will decrease intrinsic values on a penny for penny basis, and some options will move to zero intrinsic value as the movement continues.

The theoretical effect of a downward share price movement on put options which initially have no intrinsic value (because the share price is above the striking price) is shown in Figure 9.2(a). At some point the downward price movement takes the share price below the striking price, at which point the graph takes on a slope of 45 degrees, i.e. the increase is on a penny for penny basis with the price fall.

The effect of an upward share price movement on a put option which initially has an intrinsic value because the share price is below the striking price is

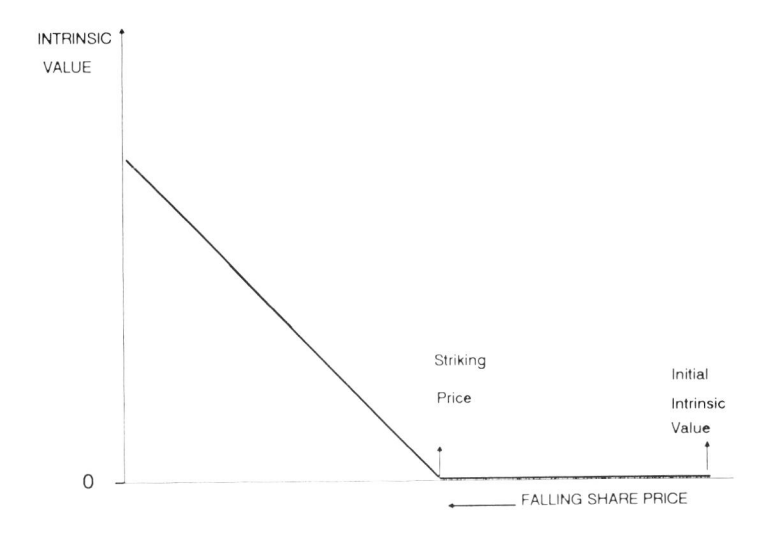

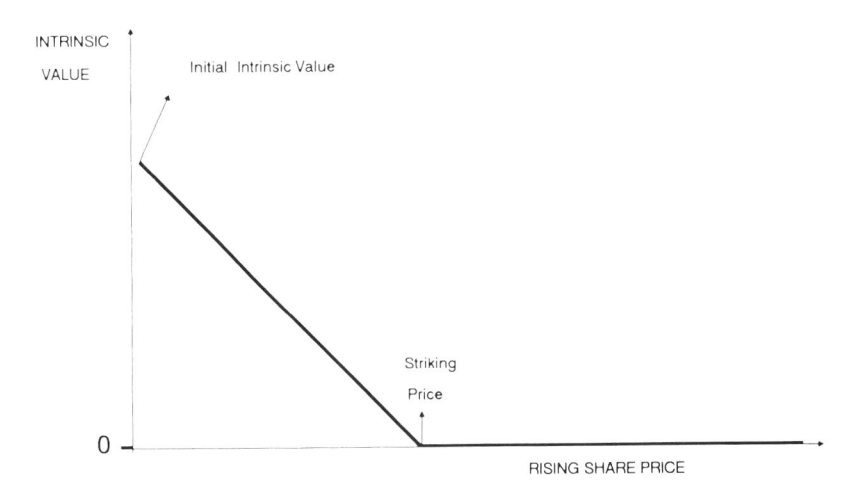

Figure 9.2. (a) Effect of downward share price movement on put options with no initial intrinsic value (b) effect of upward share price movement on put options which have an initial intrinsic value.

shown in Figure 9.2(b). Here the line falls at a slope of 45 degrees due to the penny for penny fall in option value with rise in share price. Once the share price and striking price become equal, the intrinsic value becomes zero and stays so with increasing share price.

Time Values

Time values are not based on a direct mathematical relationship as is the case with intrinsic values. Time values are simply decided by the balance between purchasers and writers of options, which itself depends upon the view of the future that each of these classes of investor have. We might expect the following reactions in time values for the various share price movements:

1. A static share price should certainly not cause time values to rise. The normal behaviour with no share price movement is for put option premiums to stay more or less constant until about six weeks before the expiry of the option, at which point the time values will fall off rapidly, becoming zero at expiry.

2. A downward share price movement should have a positive effect on time values, with the greatest effect being on the more distant expiry dates. We have already stated that the normal tendency with a neutral share price is for time values to decrease over the last six weeks of the option's life, and therefore we would expect that the positive effect of the downward share price movement is to cancel this normal decrease, leaving options with say six to eight weeks to expiry having virtually static time values. Options with only one or two weeks to expiry will require a very substantial share price fall to offset the disappearing time value.

Table 9.2. Movement of Dixons Share and Option Prices from 12/2/88 to 11/3/88 (Time Values in [ ])

Item		12/2/88	19/2/88	27/2/88	4/3/88	11/3/88
Share		180	187	187	185	184
MAR	180s	8[8]	4[4]	4[4]	3[3]	3[3]
	200s	28[8]	18[5]	16[3]	17[2]	18[2]
	220s	45[5]	36[3]	34[1]	36[1]	38[2]
JUN	180s	16[16]	11[11]	10[10]	9[9]	9[9]
	200s	30[10]	25[12]	23[10]	22[7]	24[8]
	220s	45[5]	38[5]	34[1]	36[1]	38[2]
SEP	180s	23[23]	15[15]	13[13]	14[14]	13[13]
	200s	35[15]	30[17]	26[13]	26[11]	28[12]
	220s	48[8]	44[11]	40[7]	38[3]	42[6]

Table 9.3. Movement of Thorn-EMI Share and Put Option Prices from 8/1/88 to 5/2/88 (Time Values in [ ])

Item		8/1/88	15/1/88	22/1/88	30/1/88	5/2/88
Share		564	572	570	574	567
MAR	500s	15[15]	12[12]	10[10]	9[9]	5[5]
	550s	27[27]	23[23]	25[25]	18[18]	16[16]
	600s	54[18]	45[17]	48[18]	47[21]	45[12]
JUN	500s	22[22]	20[20]	18[18]	18[18]	18[18]
	550s	40[40]	40[40]	37[37]	37[37]	38[38]
	600s	62[26]	63[35]	64[34]	63 [37]	67[34]
SEP	500s	30[30]	30[30]	28[28]	30[30]	30[30]
	550s	55[55]	50[50]	47[47]	50[50]	55[55]
	600s	-	72[44]	70[40]	77[41]	87[54]

3. *An upward share price movement should have the most effect on the time value of those options nearest to expiry, making them fall even more rapidly than if the share price is static. This is because there is little time left for the trend to reverse direction. Where options have more distant expiry dates we would expect little effect unless the upward share price move increases in momentum.*

As in the case of call options, we have to illustrate these various scenarios by means of concrete examples. It is advantageous to use the same examples as were used for call options, since besides illustrating the trends in put option time values, it gives us the additional chance of comparing the trends in the put options with the trends in the call options.

1. Static Share Prices - Dixons and Thorn-EMI Put Options

A neutral share price behaviour provide the best circumstances in which to investigate the relationship between share price and the time values of put options, and we can use the same examples as in Chapter 7. Taking Dixons first of all, during the period between 12th February and 11th March 1988 the share price moved only between the limits of 180 and 187p. The behaviour of the time values is shown in Table 9.2.

Our theoretical consideration of the effect of a static share price was that time values would remain more or less constant, but fall off during the last few weeks of the life of the option. Dixons behaved in exemplary fashion as far as

Table 9.4. Movement of Woolworth Share and Put Option Prices from 20/11/87 to 18/12/87 (Time Values in [ ])

Item		20/11/87	27/11/87	4/12/87	11/12/87	18/12/87
Share		287	269	240	261	239
JAN	280s	25[25]	35[24]	45[5]	30[11]	40[0]
APR	280s	35[35]	40[29]	52[12]	40[21]	70[29]
JUL	280s	40[40]	47[36]	60[20]	45[26]	80[39]

Table 9.5. Movement of BAA Share and Put Option Prices from 20/11/87 to 18/12/87 (Time Values in [ ])

Item		20/11/87	27/11/87	4/12/87	11/12/87	18/12/87
Share		104	93	85	96	98
Feb	90	12[12]	11[11]	13[8]	6 [6]	7[7]
	100	15[15]	18[11]	21[6]	12[8]	12[10]
May	90	15[15]	14[14]	16[11]	12[12]	10[10]
	100	19[19]	21[14]	23[8]	18[14]	16[14]
Aug	90	-	18[18]	19[14]	15[15]	13[13]
	100	22[22]	24[17]	27[12]	21[17]	19[17]

time values are concerned. Even the long expiry options behaved in the same way. In Chapter 7 we saw that the time values of Dixons call options also fell in this way with the exception of the longer expiry September options, where time values remained static.

Where the nearest expiry date of the options is rather further away, we might expect slightly different behaviour. A good example here is Thorn-EMI from 8th January to 5th February 1988. The data for these put options is given in Table 9.3.

Even though there were still two months remaining to expiry, the March options still showed a fall off in time values. Of the longer expiry June and September options, the 500s (out-of-the-money) stayed more or less constant while the September 600s (in-the-money) showed a gain in time values. It can also be clearly seen that, just like the call options, those put options closest to being at-the-money, in this case the 550s, have the highest time values, followed by the out-of-the-money options.

BUYING PUT OPTIONS   133

Table 9.6. General conclusions on the effect of a share price fall on time values and intrinsic values of put options.

Type of option	Effect on intrinsic value	Effect on time value
Short term in-the-money	rise	large fall
Short term out-of-the-money	stays zero	uncertain, medium fall or rise
Medium term in-the-money	rise	medium fall
Medium term out-of-the-money	stays zero	uncertain
Long term in-the-money	rise	medium fall
Long term out-of-the-money	stays zero	uncertain

2. Falling Share Price - Woolworths Put Options

The buyer of a call option naturally has the view that the share price will fall, and so the behaviour of put options under such circumstances is of prime importance. Since we used Woolworths as an example of a falling share price in Chapter 7, we can see the effect of this fall on the Woolworths put options between 20th November 1987 and 18th December 1987, when the share price fell from 287p to 239p, i.e. a fall of 16.7 percent. The data are given in Table 9.4.

Just as the prediction we made for the effect of a rising share price on the time values of call options in Chapter 7 was incorrect, so is the prediction we

Table 9.7. Movement of Courtaulds Share and Put Option Prices from 12/2/88 to 11/3/88 (Time Values in [ ])

Item		12/2/88	19/2/88	26/2/88	4/3/88	11/3/88
Share		307	302	312	331	317
APR	300s	12[12]	12[12]	10[10]	6[6]	8[8]
	330s	30[7]	33[5]	27[9]	14[14]	20[7]
	360s	55[2]	60[2]	50[2]	35[6]	45[2]
JUL	300s	25[25]	25[25]	20[20]	14[14]	20[20]
	330s	42[19]	45[17]	37[19]	28[28]	35[22]
	360s	67[10]	70[12]	62[14]	48[19]	58[15]
OCT	300s	27[27]	28[28]	23[23]	18[18]	20[20]
	330s	45[22]	47[19]	40[22]	30[30]	37[24]
	360s	67[14]	68[10]	62[14]	50 [21]	58[15]

134 TRADED OPTIONS SIMPLIFIED

Table 9.8. Movement of Trafalgar House Share and Put Option Prices from 12/2/88 to 11/3/88 (Time Values in [ ])

Item		12/2/88	19/2/88	26/2/88	4/3/88	11/3/88
Share		322	317	329	346	325
APR	300s	8[8]	8[8]	7[7]	3[3]	3[3]
	330s	20[19]	22[9]	17[16]	7[7]	15[10]
	360s	43[5]	48[5]	37[6]	22[8]	40[5]
JUL	300s	18[18]	17[17]	12[12]	7[7]	13[13]
	330s	33[25]	30[17]	25[24]	16[16]	27[22]
	360s	52[14]	55[12]	43[12]	32[18]	47[12]
OCT	300s	22[22]	20[20]	15[15]	10[10]	18[18]
	330s	37[29]	35[22]	28[27]	22[22]	32[27]
	360s	58[20]	58[15]	48[17]	38[24]	53[18]

made here for put option time values with a falling share price. The time values do not rise - they either fall, or at best remain static even with a share price fall of 16%. The loss of time value is severest for the near expiry January options, less so for the medium term April options and negligible for the longer expiry July options.

Taking a share which showed a more modest fall over the same time period, British Airports Authority, we have the data given in Table 9.5. Note once again the failure of time values to behave quite as we predicted. Perhaps the most illogical change in time value was that occurring between 27th November and 4th December. The share price fell by 8p, so naturally we expect the premium to reflect this move in the right direction by rising. The rise in the premium was quite small, between 1p and 3p, but the interesting fact was that the time values actually fell. This is the same effect that we noticed in Chapter 7 when discussing the behaviour of the time values of call options at a time when the share price was moving favourably. Just as we did for call options, we can make some general conclusions about the effect on time values and intrinsic values of put options when the share price falls. This is shown in Table 9.6.

The only constant effect which can be seen across a wide range of put options is that the short term, in-the-money options show large falls in their time values when the share price falls. One reason for this may be that investors become less certain that a fall occurring over the space of a few weeks will continue, and more certain that it will reverse direction.

BUYING PUT OPTIONS

Table 9.9. Expected gains, on a scale of 1 to 5, for various put options when the share price falls.

in-the-money	+ + +	+ +	+
at-the-money	+ + + +	+ + +	+ +
out-of-the-money	+ + + + +	+ + + +	+ + +
	short	medium	long

Table 9.10. Approximate level of premiums for various put options.

in-the-money	+ + +	+ + + +	+ + + + +
at-the-money	+ +	+ + +	+ + + +
out-of-the-money	+	+ +	+ + +
	short	medium	long

3. Rising Share Price - Courtaulds and Trafalgar House

In our theoretical discussion of time values, we came to the conclusion that a rising share price should cause a rapid erosion of the time values of the options of nearest expiry, because of the lack of time for the adverse trend to reverse itself.

As we can see, Courtaulds April 300s, i.e. out-of-the-money options did show a considerable fall in time values, but paradoxically the other two April in-the-money options showed a rise in time values as their intrinsic values fell. Probably the only obvious correlation is that time values are highest for those options whose striking price is closest to the share price itself, i.e. are close to being at-the-money.

The Trafalgar House options behaved slightly more rationally than Courtaulds, the time values of all of the out-of-the-money 300s falling considerably by 4th March. The longer term 330s saw modest falls in time values, while the in-the-money 360s all showed modest rises by the same date.

Potential for Profit and Loss

As was the case with call options, the discussion on intrinsic values and time values for shares which are falling, static or rising is intended to provide a background to the selection of the correct option. The list of options will of course have been greatly reduced by the use of correlation, as discussed in

Table 9.11. Gains made in in-the-money put options in the two weeks from 20/8/88 to 3/9/88.

Share	20th August 1988				3rd September 1988				Sep Gain	Dec Gain	Mar Gain	Share Gain
	Strike Price	Share Price	Sep Prm	Dec Prm	Mar Pr	Sep Prm	Dec Prm	Mar Prm	Share Prce			
Beecham	500	477	28	35	39	39	44	48	463	39.3	25.7	23.1	-2.94
Blue Circle	460	457	23	32	38	46	48	52	421	100.0	50.0	36.8	-7.88
Dixons	180	181	7	11	13	31	33	35	150	342.9	200.0	169.2	-17.13
Glaxo	1000	986	50	73	80	52	75	85	956	4.0	2.7	6.3	-1.24
Hawker	550	521	38	45	50	53	60	65	506	39.5	33.3	30.0	-2.88
Hillsdown	300	286	18	23	28	42	42	42	260	133.3	82.6	50.0	-9.09
Hanson	160	144	17.5	19	19.5	21	22	22	140	20.0	15.8	12.8	-2.78
Lonrho	260	248	17	20	26	14	16	23	250	-17.6	-20.0	-11.5	0.81
Midland	420	415	14	18	27	30	30	40	391	114.3	66.7	48.1	-5.78
Tesco	160	148	13	16	16	22	22	23	140	69.2	37.5	43.8	-5.41
THF	260	253	12	16	22	28	30	34	233	133.3	87.5	54.5	-7.91
Thorn-EMI	700	666	38	47	50	80	80	82	622	110.5	70.2	64.0	-6.61
Unilever	460	457	15	22	28	23	31	34	440	53.3	40.9	21.4	-3.72
Unilever	500	457	45	48	51	62	65	66	440	37.8	35.4	29.4	-3.72
Average Gains										84.27	52.03	41.28	-5.45

Chapter 5, so that attention now has to turn to two other aspects. These are the gap between share price and striking price, i.e. the extent to which the option lies in- or out-of-the-money, and the length of time remaining to expiry, i.e. whether the option is of short, medium or long term expiry.

Using these three expiry terms and three degrees of gap between share price and striking price, we can arrive at the three by three matrix shown in Table 9.9. The gains here are based on the share price moving in the direction anticipated by the buyer of call options, i.e. downwards and are given on a scale of 1 to 5, and must be considered very approximate. There will be many exceptions, but the overall picture given by Table 9.9 is helpful.

The potential for the largest gain in the option price lies with the out-of-the-money options which are short term to expiry, while the longer term expiry, in-the-money options have the least potential for gain.

As far as losses are concerned when the share price rises rather than falls, then very approximately, these are directly proportional to the gain made when the share price falls, i.e. the higher the potential for profit, the higher is the potential for loss. The obvious deduction from this is that the short term, out-of-the-money options are the riskiest while the long term, in-the-money options are the safest. This ignores the actual premiums which are being paid,

BUYING PUT OPTIONS 137

Table 9.12. Gains in the out-of-the-money put options

Share	Strike Price	20th August 1988						3rd September 1988			Sep Gain	Dec Gain	Mar Gain	Share Gain
		Share Price	Sep Prm	Dec Prm	Mar Prm	Sep Prm	Dec Prm	Mar Prm	Share Price					
Beecham	460	477	7	15	19	9	20	24	463	28.57	33.33	26.32	-2.94
Blue Circ	420	457	6	13	18	14	22	26	421	133.33	69.23	44.44	-7.88
Dixons	160	181	1.5	3	5	13	16	19	150	766.67	433.33	280.00	-17.13
Glaxo	950	968	20	45	55	20	48	57	956	0.00	6.67	3.64	-1.24
Hawker	460	521	3	5	9	3	7	13	506	0.00	40.00	44.44	-2.88
Hawker	500	521	9	18	25	15	25	33	506	66.67	38.89	32.00	-2.88
Hillsdown	260	286	2	5	7	7	11	15	260	250.00	120.00	114.29	-9.09
Hillsdown	280	286	7	10	14	22	23	27	260	214.29	130.00	92.86	-9.09
Hanson	130	146	1.7	2.5	3.5	0.7	3	4.5	140	-57.14	20.00	28.57	-2.78
Hanson	140	144	2.5	6.2	7.5	3.2	7.25	8.25	140	30.00	16.00	10.00	-2.78
Lonrho	240	248	5	9	15	3	7	14	250	-40.00	-22.22	-6.67	0.81
Midland	390	415	3	7	-	9	14	20	391	20	0.00	100.00	-5.78
Tesco	140	148	2	5	6	5	9	10	140	150.00	80.00	66.67	-5.41
THF	240	253	3	7	12	10	15	20	233	233.33	114.29	66.67	-7.91
Thorn-EMI	600	666	1.5	6	12	7	14	20	622	366.67	133.33	66.67	-6.61
Thorn-EMI	650	666	7	20	27	33	38	47	622	371.43	90.00	74.07	-6.61
Unilever	420	457	3	8	12	3	11	14	440	0.00	37.50	16.67	-3.72
Unilever	460	457	15	2	28	23	31	34	440	53.33	40.91	21.43	-3.72
						Average gains				153.73	82.29	57.77	-5.31

because the amount of money being risked is also important. The usual levels of premium level associated with these various categories of options are shown in Table 9.10

From this is can be seen that the investor in short expiry, in-the-money options is risking far more capital than an investor going for out-of-the-money options, so this point should always be borne in mind when considering the risk/reward relationship for a particular option.

When to buy in-the-money put options

The above discussion shows that the profit potential of in-the-money put options is always less than that of the out-of-the-money counterparts. However, Table 9.11, which shows the gains made in put options over the two week period from 20th August 1988 to 3rd September 1988 illustrates quite clearly that these gains are quite large when set against the movement in the share prices. Thus for the options listed, the share prices averages a fall of 5.45%, whereas the average gain made in the near expiry September options was 84.27%, the medium expiry December options 52.03% and the longer expiry March options 41.28%. The gearing achieved by these options was a factor of 15.5 for September, 9.5 for December and 7.6 for March put options. By any standards therefore in-the-money put options can be considered to be an excellent investment vehicle for investors who consider that the share price trend is to show a modest fall over a fairly short time period.

Just as was the case with call options, a key to improving even the large profit potential that exists with put options is to try to find those options which have time values much too low for the circumstances. These anomalous options are most likely to be found in the short-expiry series. One obvious example is Tesco, where at a share price of 148p on 20th August, the premium of 13p for the September 160 puts included only 1p for the time value. By 17th September, the share price had fallen to 133p and the September 160s had risen to 30p, for a profit of 130% in just one month.

Out-of-the-money options

These options offer the investor a higher return than their in-the-money counterparts, but of course at the cost of a higher risk of loss, even though the absolute level of premium at risk is lower. The investor in out-of-the-money options must be as sure as he can be that the trend of the share price is for a considerable fall over the time remaining to expiry of the option. There are two prime considerations:

1. Only take out put options which are substantially out-of-the-money in shares which are at the top of the volatility league. This is because a considerable fall in share price is necessary to put such options into an in-the-money position with intrinsic value. Involatile shares often move so slowly that they have not reached the striking price by expiry time.

2. The question as to which to invest in of the short, medium or long term expiry options has to depend upon a firm prediction as to the timescale of the anticipated share price fall. This is best carried out by means of channel analysis, so that the expiry date can then be chosen so as to coincide as near as is possible with the lowest share price that will be attained.

The gains achieved in the corresponding out-of-the-money options to those given in Table 9.11 are shown in Table 9.12 over the same time period from 20th August to 3rd September 1988. The gains made in the short term September options are nearly twice those made in the in-the-money options of the same shares, while the longer expiry options made returns about 50% higher.

Tired Options

As the share price continues to fall, the gains being made on a week by week basis in an option will start to decrease. This is especially noticeable in those options with the nearest expiry dates. One reason for this behaviour is that, as we have discussed previously, the time values of options start to decrease rapidly over the last six weeks or so of the life of the option, so this tends to reduce the gains which are being made. Also, the opinion of investors themselves will be that a downward trend in share prices which has continued for any length of time will certainly come to an end, and therefore demand for put options will start to decrease, thereby having a braking effect on the value of the premium. Just as was the case with call options, the investor who thinks that the share price trend will continue for some time to come should close the present position and open another one in a different put option of the same share by rolling down the options.

SUBSEQUENT ACTION

As with call options, once a put option has been purchased, then the position must be monitored constantly to see that the downtrend in share price expected when you bought the option is maintained. Two outcomes require that you take action different from that which you intended when you bought the option. The first is a rise in share price, while the second is when the downward trend in the share price appears to be developing into something much more significant or sustained than was first envisaged. In this case you may wish to benefit even more from this movement than your present position allows.

Rising Share Price

There are basically two actions that you can take if the share price begins to move adversely. If you feel that the downward trend that was the reason for the purchase of the put option has now ended prematurely, then the position should be closed. If, on the other hand, you feel that this new rise in price is just a temporary blip, and you are still of the opinion that the real underlying trend is still downwards, then you could just hold the position, waiting for the original movement to be re-established. There is a less risky alternative to this, and that is the strategy of rolling down.

Rolling Down the Options

This is the strategy to employ if you are quite sure that the downwards price movement of the share price will continue and wish to continue to increase your profit on its upwards trend, but see the current option as becoming tired. You have to be as sure as is possible about the share price trend continuing, because you are putting at risk the profit you have already accumulated, and expecting a share price trend which may have continued for some time to continue for a further period. The strategy is called 'rolling down' because you sell an option and move to a new option with a lower striking price than previously.

There is one major criterion can be used to determine when to switch to an option with a lower strike price. This is when the share price has fallen so as to put the current option from an out-of-the-money position with no intrinsic value to a position which is close to being at-the-money. Of course, this only applies if you started with an option which is out-of-the-money. If that is not the case, then stay with your in-the-money option until there are only a few weeks to expiry before moving into a different option.

The new option to move into is the one that is furthest out-of-the-money, which of course will be a new option introduced by the authorities to maintain the balance of striking prices around the share price (see Chapter 2).

Our strategy is therefore:

1. Sell once the share price has reached the striking price or thereabouts, or if the option was initially in-the-money, sell when only a few weeks are left to expiry.

2. Buy the furthest out-of-the-money option with the nearest expiry date that gives you at least a further six weeks to expiry.

This strategy will bring the maximum gearing and therefore the maximum profit during the course of the predicted share price fall. We have already said that once this strategy has been under way for some time, the amount of risk involved is high, and the number of contracts which have been bought will have grown rapidly. It is absolutely essential that all techniques at the disposal of the investor to predict the end of the downward share price trend should, be utilised, including of course channel analysis.

CHAPTER 10

Writing Put Options

The writer of a put option receives a premium from a buyer of the option and in return has undertaken to buy the shares at the striking price if a buyer exercises the option.

The writer of a put option is of course at the opposite side of the transaction from the purchaser of a put option. The put option buyer is bearish for the future trend of the share price, and can select a put option which reflects the degree of his bearishness and the risk he is prepared to take. The writer, on the other hand, expects primarily a rise in share price, but depending on how far in- or out-of-the money the particular option is, can also make a profit if the share price remains static or even falls slightly. Just like the writer of call options, the writer of put options has no control over if or when the option might be exercised against him; the decision on exercise rests entirely with the buyer of the option.

The objective of the writer of puts is to receive the premium available by writing, and may also be to be able to buy the shares at a lower price than the present market price. In the latter case of course the writer will acquire the shares at a real cost of the striking price less the premium received plus dealing costs, which usually turns out to be less than the striking price. Both of these objectives imply a bullish nature for the writer. He is prepared to receive the shares because he then expects them to rise to make a profit.

In the case of call option writers, we had two categories: the naked call writer, who did not own the shares corresponding to the option being written and the covered writer who did own the shares. In theory it is possible to have two categories of put option writer: the naked put writer who has no position in the underlying shares themselves, and the covered put writer, who has sold the underlying shares but has yet to deliver them. He would be covered in the sense that if the shares are put to him, he needed them to fulfil his commitment in the shares themselves. Covered put writing is a perfectly viable proposition in the United States markets, where it is possible to go short on shares, i.e. sell them without delivering them, for long periods of time provided the seller puts up a sufficient margin. In the U.K. however, it is difficult to carry such a short position for more than one Stock Exchange account, and therefore in this treatment of put option writing, it is only the naked put writer that will be considered.

The put writer is in the position of having the potential for a limited gain and a large loss. The gain is limited because it is the premium received. The loss is large because in the worst case, the writer will have to purchase the shares at the strike price at a time when the actual share price may have fallen to just above zero.

Margin Requirements for Writing Put Options

The same comments about margin applies as for the writer of call options (see Chapter 8). The required margin is 25% of the prevailing price for the underlying share adjusted by the amount by which the option is in- or out-of-the-money. The margin of course increases as the share price falls, thereby moving against the writer.

Exercise of Put Options

In the case of call options, the upside profit potential is limited by exercise of the option, and therefore such exercise is against the interests of the writer. On the other hand, the exercise of a put option may be the very outcome that the writer desires, since it can give him the shares at greatly reduced cost compared with that prevailing at the time he writes the option. It has already been pointed out (Chapter 8) that options are seldom exercised early in their lifetime since the initial objective of the purchaser is to see an increase in the premium value of the options rather than become involved with the shares themselves. The put option writer with the objective of acquiring the shares may thus have to wait until the last few weeks before expiry of the option before seeing its exercise. It goes without saying that the put option writer must see that he has the necessary funds available at all times to cover the cost of the share acquisition, and of course an increasing proportion of these funds will be tied up by the margin requirements of the position.

Loss-Gain Potential - Large Loss, Limited Gain

As with the other options positions, we can draw a diagram to illustrate the concept of large loss and limited gain by plotting the profit or loss potential against the share price. This is shown in Figure 10.1.

At the point A, the share price is equal to the striking price of the put option, and the purchaser would be considering exercising the option. The profit, i.e. the original premium, has remained constant down to this point, but as the share price falls, the writer, if the put is exercised against him, will have to pay an increasing amount above the share price (the difference between the strike price and the share price) when accepting the shares at the exercise price. Since

WRITING PUT OPTIONS 143

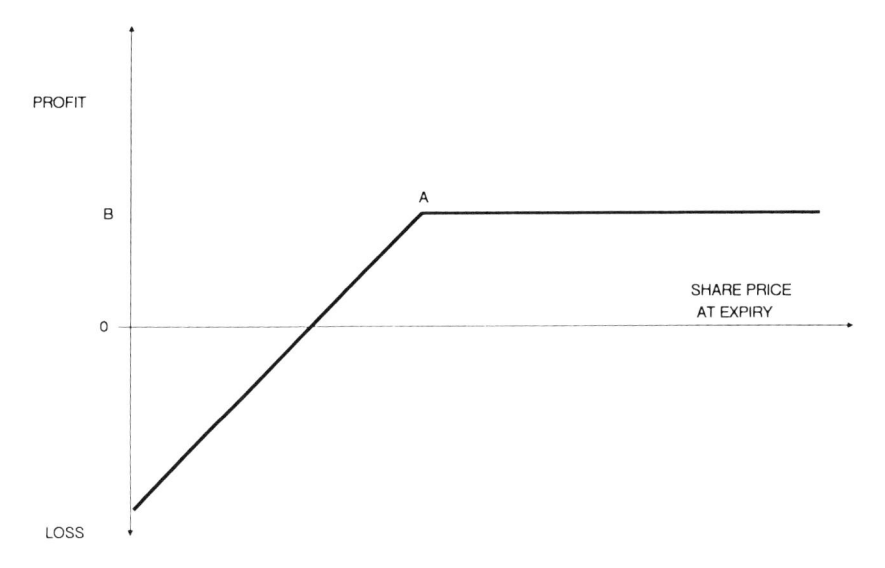

Figure 10.1. Profit/loss situation for a put writer with changing share price. The point A is the striking price and the point B is the premium received.

Table 10.1. The effect of the October Crash on put option premiums.

Item	Ex Price	Share Prce 10/10/87	Option Premiums Received (p)			Share Pr 4/10/87	Loss (p)
Courtaulds	460	513	0.5[Oct]	7[Jan]	12[Apr]	383	77
	500		6	24	28		117
	550		40	52	58		167
Trafalgar House	390	424	2	10	17	319	71
	420		8	22	30		101
	460		37	45	53		141
Woolworth	350	369	3	-	-	314	36
	360		-	-	25		46
	375		17	23	-		61
BAA	130	150	1[Nov]	4[Feb]	7[May]	116	14
	140		3.5	9	11		24
	160		14	19	22		44
Dixons	360	397	7[Dec]	15[Mar]	18[Jun]	271	89
	390		18	24	30		119
	420		34	-	-		149
Thorn-EMI	650	719	7	20	25	533	117
	700		22	32	42		167
	750		50	53	65		217

144 TRADED OPTIONS SIMPLIFIED

the share price can go all the way down to a point marginally above zero, the maximum loss that can be sustained is marginally less than the strike price at which the put options were written.

Although the novice put writer may be of the opinion that share price falls may be of limited extent, so that the potential loss is not all that large, it is worth drawing attention once again to Black October to show what effect share price falls of 20 to 30% magnitude can have on a put option writer. As example we can take the various options used as examples so far in this book: Dixons, Thorn-EMI, Courtaulds, Trafalgar House, Woolworths and BAA, and these are shown in Table 10.1. The smallest loss is 14p for each BAA share against a premium received of 1p, while the largest loss is 217p for each Thorn-EMI share against a premium received of 50p. Expressed as a ratio, the loss in the case of BAA is fourteen times the amount of premium received, while the loss in the case of Thorn-EMI is four times the premium received. Since option writers usually write a sufficient number of contracts to make the premium received a useful sum, it can be seen that the losses, especially in the case of BAA are horrendous. This is not to suggest that the writing of put options should be avoided, but to emphasise that the writer must be aware at all times of the risk, and stay within sensible limits of exposure. Even share price falls of lesser momentum than those on Black Monday can pose a difficulty, and the writer should always be prepared to close the position at the first sign that things are not going to plan.

The potential for gain for the put option writer is of course simply the value of the premium received, less dealing costs. The potential for loss depends upon three factors: the premium, the striking price and the share price prevailing at the time of exercise. The relationship is:

LOSS = PREMIUM RECEIVED(A) - STRIKING PRICE(B)
       + SHARE PRICE(C)

The potential for gain or loss can be summed up in Table 10.2.

Table 10.2. Potential for gain/loss for put options

Type of option	A	- B + C	Result
In-the-money	* * *	negative	loss
At-the-money	* *	zero	gain (= A)
Out-of-the-money	*	positive	gain (= A)

WRITING PUT OPTIONS 145

Table 10.3. Profit from various Courtaulds April put options where share price is 331p.

Type of option		If exercised	If not exercised
In-the-money	360s	35 + 331 - 360 = 6	35
At-the-money	330s	would not be exercised	14
Out-of-the-money	300s	would not be exercised	6

If the at-the-money and out-of-the-money options stay that way until expiry, they will not be exercised and therefore the gain is equal to the premium (A). As we saw previously from Figure 10.1, the loss can increase to a maximum where the share price is just above zero, and this is therefore the potential for loss which the writer has to take into account when deciding on his course of action. These various scenarios are best described by an actual example, Courtaulds on 4th March 1988:

Share price 331p April 300s, 6p; 330s, 14p; 360s, 35p July 300s, 14p; 330s, 28p; 360s, 48p October300s, 18p; 330s, 30p; 360s, 50p

Taking just the April options, the profit from the options (ignoring dealing expenses) at expiry are shown in Table 10.3.

By the convention of the last chapter, the upside potential in the writing of these April put options is the value found in the final column, i.e. 35p, 14p or 6p, while the downside potential is the value found in the 'If exercised' column. At the date at which the data was taken, then obviously with a share price of 331p the at-the-money and out-of-the-money options would not be exercised. The downside potential at the time was to limit the gain to 6p, which in real terms, taking into account dealing expenses could mean a small loss.

The position for the various categories of put option writing can be summarised as:

In-the-money put option writing: good potential on the upside
very high potential for loss
At-the-money put option writing: moderate potential on the upside
high potential for loss

Out-of-the-money put option writing: poor potential on the upside
fairly high potential for loss

As one would expect therefore, options with the highest potential for gain are also those with the highest potential for loss. The more conservative put

146   TRADED OPTIONS SIMPLIFIED

Table 10.4. Premiums per month remaining to expiry for the options listed in Table 7.1. The data is for 26th February 1988.

Option		Expiry Month	Premium P/Month	Expiry Month	Premium P/Month	Expiry Month	Premium P/Month
Dixons	180	March	4.0	June	2.5	September	1.9
	200		16.0		5.8		3.7
	220		34.0		8.5		5.7
Trafalgar	300	April	3.5	July	2.4	October	1.9
	330		8.5		5.0		3.5
	360		18.5		8.6		6.0
Brit. Tel	220	May	1.2	August	1.3	November	1.3
	240		3.2		2.7		2.0
	260		6.3		4.3		3.3

option writer would tend to favour the out-of-the-money options, accepting the lower profit potential in return for the lower loss potential.

Timescale

It is as vital for a put option writer as it is with any other option position that he is clear about the timescale of the share price trend he is about to use to make his profit. Although some put options writers might feel relaxed about the option being exercised so that they have to take delivery of the shares themselves, most would have as their strategy the avoidance of this outcome. In this case the expiry date of the option which is being written should be nearer than the anticipated length of time for which the trend will continue. This will then ensure that the trend does not go into reverse, making exercise of the option become increasingly attractive as the adverse trend continues. Just as with the writer of call options, time is the put option writer's enemy, in the sense that since he has already pocketed the premium, the sooner the option expires worthless the better. On the other hand the buyer of the put option may consider that it is worth paying extra for time since even if the share price moves against him initially, this may change in his favour as time goes on. The writer is faced with a simple choice - either to take the higher premium associated with the further out expiry dates and also accept a higher risk of events moving against him, or take the lower premium for the shorter expiry options where the risk of adverse movement of share price is much less.

More light can be thrown on this aspect of put option writing if the premiums are expressed as a weekly return (WR). We can take the data for Dixons, Trafalgar House and British Telecom for the 26th February 1988 which is given in Table 10.4.. Quite obviously, within a particular option class, the further out the expiry date, the less is the premium per month remaining. The buyer of a put options is therefore reducing his costs per month by going for the longer expiry options. On the other hand, the writers of put options will receive less premium per month for these longer expiry options, i.e. his WR is less. Thus, unless there are vary valid reasons for the contrary, the writer is better off going for the shorter expiry options.

As with call options, the two major considerations of interest to the option writer will be those situations where there may be anomalous time values, and those where the CPP values are high.

Anomalous Time Values

The purchaser of a put option can frequently spot an anomalous situation where the time value is much too small for the amount of time remaining to the expiry of the option. In the last Chapter we drew attention to the Tesco September 160 puts, where the time value was only 1p on 20th August with more than four weeks to go until expiry. As far as the put option writer is concerned, this situation has to be avoided, since the premium received will be less than is usual for such an option at that stage of its life. The writer has to take an opposite view, looking for anomalous situations where the time values are too high for the circumstances. In such cases the writer will then receive a higher than usual premium without taking on board any higher risk. Note that time values are highest for those options which are closest to being at-the-money.

Since we have indicated that the short expiry options are the most sensible for the writer, then these are the ones which should be scanned for anomalies. As an example, we can take the premiums for the out-of-the-money short expiry June puts (where the premiums will be equal to the time value) on 18th March 1988 and 1st April 1988. These are shown in Table 10.5.

Of this list of eighteen shares and option premiums, only five shares did not rise in price between the two dates in April. The anomalies we should look for in such a situation are where the time values do not fall substantially in spite of a either a rise in share price, or a very modest fall in share price. Two such situations can be seen in Table 10.3. The Blue Circle premium held fairly well although the share price remained steady, and the Wellcome 420 options were still at at useful premium even though the share price rose considerably. The premiums which these two options commanded, 15p, and 11p represented very good writing opportunities at a time when, in the absence of any other evidence, the share price were either rising, or at worst remaining steady, i.e. at a time therefore when the risk appeared to favour the writer. At expiry, the share prices were 423p for Blue Circle and 542p for Wellcome, so that the options expired worthless from the point of view of the purchaser.

148 TRADED OPTIONS SIMPLIFIED

Table 10.5. Premiums and share prices for June options on 1st and 15th April 1988.

Share	Series	Striking Price	1st April 1988		15th April 1988	
			Premium	Share Price	Premium	Share Price
Amstrad	Jun	140	6	155	4	157
Barclays	Jun	460	17	475	40	425
Beecham	Jun	420	7	456	6	460
Boots	Jun	200	7	213	3	223
BTR	Jun	240	13	238	8	246
Blue Circle	Jun	420	20	441	15	441
Dixons	Jun	160	7	172	4	176
Glaxo	Jun	950	33	992	35	972
Hawker	Jun	460	28	472	37	451
Hanson	Jun	120	4.5	124	3.25	126
Lonrho	Jun	220	7	233	5	241
Midland Bnk	Jun	360	10	385	8	391
Sears	Jun	120	6	124	5	127
Tesco	Jun	140	5	152	5	152
THF	Jun	220	7	234	4	235
Thorn-EMI	Jun	550	15	576	5	608
Unilever	Jun	420	7	462	7	458
Wellcome	Jun	420	19	444	11	457

It is worthwhile comparing these two options on the basis of upside and downside potential. For Blue Circle, the situation is:
Upside Potential: 15p (the premium)
Downside Potential: 420p (the striking price you will have to pay if exercised when shares are valueless)
U/D ratio = 0.036

For Wellcome, the situation is:
Upside Potential: 11p
Downside Potential: 420p
U/D ratio = 0.026

As far as the U/D ratio is concerned, the Blue Circle example is slightly more favourable to the writer.

The above examples of course take the very simplistic view that the behaviour in share prices over a two week period nearly two months before the expiry of the options is a good indicator of their behaviour over the rest of the period to expiry. As we have continued to stress in this book, it is imperative

Table 10.6. CPP values calculated for various June options on 15th April 1988, with share prices at expiry of the options.

Share	Expiry	Ex Price	15th April 1988 Premium	Share Price	CPP	Share price at expiry
Amstrad	Jun	140	4	157	0.299	206
Barclays	Jun	460	40	425	34.0	410
Beecham	Jun	420	6	460	0.6	469
Boots	Jun	200	3	223	0.26	220
BTR	Jun	240	8	246	1.41	267
Blue Circle	Jun	420	15	441	1.84	423
Dixons	Jun	160	4	176	0.35	186
Glaxo	Jun	950	35	972	5.97	933
Hawker	Jun	460	37	451	5.96	502
Hanson	Jun	120	3.25	126	0.44	137
Lonrho	Jun	220	5	241	0.46	240
Midland Bnk	Jun	360	8	391	0.8	428
Sears	Jun	120	5	127	0.53	119
Tesco	Jun	140	5	152	0.45	147
THF	Jun	220	4	235	0.50	243
Thorn-EMI	Jun	550	5	608	0.48	661
Unilever	Jun	420	7	458	0.71	476
Wellcome	Jun	420	11	457	1.05	542

that you hold a clear view of the predicted price movement of the shares in which you are interested before taking any option position. In the case of Wellcome, this would have shown that, on 15th April, the price was just approaching a minor trough, and therefore the price could be expected to

150 TRADED OPTIONS SIMPLIFIED

rebound upwards. On the basis of such predictions, writing of put options in both Blue Circle and Wellcome would be low risk positions.

Cost Per Percentage Point (CPP)

We have discussed earlier in Chapter 5 the method of calculating CPPs for put options. We saw then that buyers of put options should look for those with low CPPs. Since writers of put options are diametrically opposed, they should avoid those options with low CPPs and look for options with high CPPs. The CPPs are calculated for the same options as are listed in Table 10.5 taking the data for 15th April 1988 and are shown in Table 10.6. Also shown are the share prices at the expiry date of these June options.

Note that the Barclays option had moved into an in-the-money situation by 15th April, and so the CPP is out of line with the out-of-the-money options. To a lesser extent the same comment applies to Hawker Siddeley. Of the other fourteen entries in the Table, the top seven were Glaxo, Blue Circle, BTR, Wellcome, Midland Bank and Beecham. As a reasonable approach therefore, it would be wise to select the options for writing out of this list, applying in addition any further criteria. It is gratifying that both Blue Circle and Wellcome appear in this list. Of the list in Table 10.4, only Barclays, Glaxo and Sears saw a fall in share price by the expiry date, so that all of the other selections would have been profitable. Of these three shares that fell in price, Sears expired only 1p below the striking price, so that it would not have been profitable for the purchaser of the put option to exercise. The Glaxo case is marginal once expenses are taken into account, so that in the real life situation, only Barclays would have been exercised against the writer, and even there, the loss to the writer would have been quite small.

SUBSEQUENT ACTION

You will have written the put option in the first place because you were bullish of the direction of the share price movement during the time remaining to expiry of the option. The two outcomes where you will have to take a decision other than continue to hold the position is when either the share price falls, or the share price rise turns into something much more significant than you first expected.

Falling Share Price

The sensible course of action here is to close your current position, protecting the profit if you have one, and limiting your loss if you have not made a profit. You should do this unless you are totally convinced that the fall in share price is purely temporary, and that the upward trend will recommence well before the expiry of the option. Two other courses of action are to maintain the current position or roll down the option. Holding the current position is the riskiest tactic with a falling share price, and it goes without saying that you require very good reasons for following this course. Less risky than this is to roll down the option

Rolling Down

Rolling down for the writer of a put option means closing the currrent option position and writing an option with a lower strike price. Naturally the risk is thereby reduced because of the lower strike price, but the potential profit is also reduced. To close the current position will of course require a net outlay over the premium you received initially, since the option premium will have risen due to the fall in the share price. This will be offset by writing the option of lower striking price. As an example, take the Woolworth put options between 27th November and 18th December.

On 27th December, with the share price at 269p, the April 280s were at a premium of 40p and appeared to be an attractive writing opportunity to the investor. By 28th December the share price had fallen to 239p, but the investor was convinced that this represented the bottom of a short term trough and that the price would change direction. The April 280s were then at a premium of 70p. The April 260s were at 50p and the 240s at 30p. Rolling down would give the following position:

Initial premium received : 40p
Upside potential is therefore 40p
Downside potential is striking price = 280p

The investor closed the initial position by buying back the option at 70p and writing a new option at a lower striking price, the April 260s.

The position is then:

Initial premium received: 40p
Less buy back of option : 70p
Plus premium from April 260s: 50p

Premium now in pocket: 40 - 70 + 50 = 20p.

Upside potential is therefore 20p
Downside potential is therefore 260p.

The investor has therefore reduced his potential for profit from 40p down to 20p, but in doing so has reduced his risk accordingly. The share price is now standing 11p below the striking price, whereas prior to rolling down, the share price was standing 31p below the original striking price, obviously placing the writer in danger of being exercised against.

Rising Share Price

Naturally, if the share price rise is in line with your original expectations, you should stay with your original objectives when you wrote the put. If the price rise looks as if it will exceed these original expecations, both in the time for which the rise will endure and its extent then you could consider rolling up to a higher striking price.

Rolling Up

This strategy should only be used if you are convinced that the share price rise will continue for a considerable period of time and you wish to maximise your profit potential from the situation. The procedure is:

1. Close the position in your current option.

2. Write an option at a higher striking price.

By rolling up, you will be closing your original position at a profit, since the premium required to close the option will be less than it was when you wrote it. You will then in addition receive another premium for writing the option at a higher striking price, although this premium may well be less than the original due to the general fall-off in put premiums against the background of the share price rise. Note though that the penalty for this improved potential for profit is an increased risk, since the potential for loss is now the new, higher striking price.

CHAPTER 11

Advanced Strategies. 1. Spreads.

So far our option strategies have involved taking a position just in one option, either by buying or writing call options or buying or writing put options. Advanced strategies require us to take positions in more than one series simultaneously. Most of these strategies involve two different series, although there are some that require three. The ability to calculate the overall profit and loss potential for an advanced strategy is vital if the strategy is to be successful, but the arithmetic used is simple, being just an extension of the methods we have used so far with simple strategies. Graphical representations are used wherever possible to illustrate the profit and loss potentials as the share price rises or falls.

Since we are taking a position in each of two option series, each of these 'legs' of the strategy will have associated with it its own upside and downside potentials. Since the major aim of advanced strategies is to reduce risk, each leg will be chosen in such a way that its upside potential outweighs the downside potential of the other leg. By this approach we avoid the problems we saw with some simple strategies where the downside risk could be virtually unlimited. Note that also in the two-legged spreads discussed in this chapter, one leg is opened by buying an option while the other leg is opened by writing an option, and therefore the cost of buying one option is partly or wholly offset by receiving the premium from the opposite transaction.

Some examples of advanced strategies which will be discussed in detail are:

Bull Spreads: Buy a call with a low striking price and write a call with a high striking price.
or: Buy a put with a low striking price and write a put with a high striking price.

Bear Spreads: Buy a call with a high striking price and write a call with a low striking price.
or: Buy a put with a high striking price and write a put with a low striking price

Calendar Spreads: Buy a put or call in a certain expiry month and take an opposing position (write a put or call at same striking price) in a later expiry month.

Butterfly Spreads: Buy a call with a low striking price and a call with a high striking price and write two calls with medium striking price.
or: the same transactions using puts.

Obviously the bull spreads and bear spreads reflect in their name the basic feeling of the investor as to the direction of the share price. On the other hand, calendar spreads can be designed to be bullish, bearish or neutral. A bullish calendar spread would use a striking price above the share price while a bearish spread would use a striking price below the share price. As you might expect, a neutral spread would use a striking price which is closest to the current share price, i.e. at-the-money.

BULL SPREADS

As we pointed out above, there are two ways of achieving a bull spread - bull call spreads and bull put spreads. The call spreads are achieved by buying a call with a low striking price and writing a call with a high striking price while the put spreads are achieved by buying a put with a low striking price and writing a put with a high striking price. Bull spreads are the strategies for those investors who are moderately bullish. They limit the risk to such an investor, but also limit the upside potential. Obviously the very bullish investor does not wish to limit his profit potential, and should therefore look more closely at simple call strategies.

Costs and Margin Requirement

Note that, if we exclude the dealing costs of the spread, the overall cost will depend upon the difference between the two premiums. In the case of a call spread you will pay this difference, since the premium for buying the low striking price call will be higher than the premium received for writing the higher striking price. In the case of a put spread you will receive this difference, since the premium you pay for the put at a lower striking price will be less than the premium you receive for writing the put at the higher striking price. As long as the number of contracts for each leg of the call spread are the same, there will be no margin requirement, since you are not in a net exposure to being called. This is not true for put spreads, since you will be in a net exposure to having the shares put to you as your writing striking price is higher than your buying striking price. The margin requirement for put spread positions is

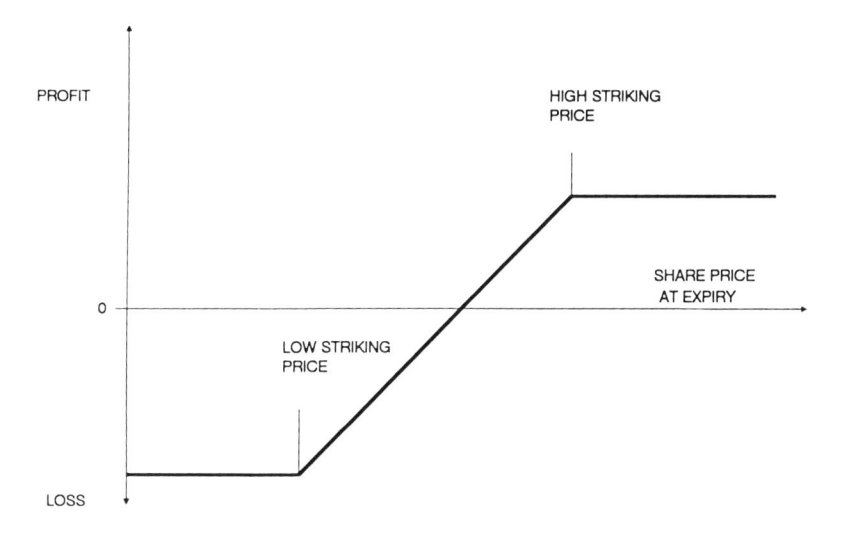

Figure 11.1. Profit and loss situation for a bull spread at expiry.

easily calculated as the difference between the two striking prices multiplied by the number of shares for which you have written contracts.

BULL CALL SPREAD

Gain-Loss Potential - Limited Gain, Limited Loss

The performance of the bull call spread for different share prices at expiry is shown in Figure 11.1. Ignoring the dealing costs, the maximum loss is simply the difference between the two premiums, i.e. your net initial outlay. This is incurred when the share price falls below the lower of the two striking prices. The maximum gain is obtained when the share price rises above the higher of the two striking prices. This profit is equal to the difference between the two striking prices less the initial capital outlay. The two changes in direction of the graph, from horizontal to upward sloping, and from upward sloping to horizontal occur at each of the two striking prices.

Although of course all bull call spreads will follow the shape of the diagram, the actual profit and loss situation will depend on the premiums and the striking prices used. As an example an investor using channel analysis on the Glaxo share price would have been moderately bullish on 3rd June (see the Glaxo chart in Chapter 8), and would have had available the following data:

Glaxo Share price: 917p
Call Option Premiums: June 850s, 73p; 900s, 30p; 950s, 7p
　　　　　　　　　　September 850s, 110p; 900s, 75p; 950s, 48p
　　　　　　　　　　December 850s, 120p; 900s, 88p; 950s, 62p

Ignoring the June options, since there are only a few weeks to go to expiry, it is possible to construct three September bull spreads and three December bull spreads out of this data:

1. Buy 850s, write 900s
2. Buy 850s, write 950s
3. Buy 900s, write 950s

As an example of the calculation for a Glaxo September bull call cpread, buying 850s @ 110p and writing 900s @ 75p:

Downside potential = difference in premiums = 110 - 75 = 35p
Upside potential = high striking price - low striking price
                            - overall premium paid
                          = 900 - 850 - 35 = 15p
U/D ratio = 15/35 = 0.43

The data on upside potential, downside potential and U/D ratio for each of these six September and December spreads is shown in Table 11.1.

Table 11.1. Upside (U) and Downside (D) Potentials for September and December Glaxo Call Spreads. The Glaxo share price is 917p.

Expiry Date	Buy 850s/Sell 900s			Buy 850s/Sell 950s			Buy 900s/Sell 950s		
	U	D	U/D	U	D	U/D	U	D	U/D
September	15	35	0.43	38	62	0.61	23	27	0.85
December	18	32	0.56	42	58	0.72	24	26	0.92

The least bullish investor, not expecting much of a price rise, would be looking at the 850/900 spread, since with a share price of 917p, i.e. above the higher of the two striking prices, the profit potential is already at its maximum. A further share price rise will not increase the profit. Both of the other two possibilities, the narrow 900/950 and the wider 850/900 spreads are equally bullish in the sense that they both require a share price rise to 950p to achieve this maximum. Where they differ is that the narrower spread has lower potential for both profit and loss. The investor simply has to make up his mind as to whether he will accept greater risk for greater reward.

BULL PUT SPREAD

Gain/Loss Potential - Limited Gain, Limited Loss

The shape of the graph for a spread using puts rather than calls is exactly the same as that shown in Figure 11.1 for calls. The maximum loss occurs when the share price falls below the lower of the two striking prices, while the maximum profit occurs when the share price rises above the higher of the two striking prices. Of course the exact values for the maximum profit and loss positions will depend on the various premiums and the spread between the striking prices. As an example, taking the Glaxo data for put options on 3rd June, we have the following data:

Glaxo Share Price: 917p
Put Option Premiums: June 850s, 1.5p; 900s, 10p; 950s, 38p
September 850s, 17p; 900s, 35p; 950s, 58p
December 850s, 29p; 900s, 48p; 950s, 75p

Ignoring the June options, since there are only a few weeks to go to expiry, it is possible to construct three September put spreads and three December put spreads out of this data:

1. Buy 850s, write 900s
2. Buy 850s, write 950s
3. Buy 900s, write 950s

As an example of the calculation for a Glaxo September put spread, buying 850s @ 17p and writing 900s @ 35p:

Downside potential = high striking price - low striking price
  - net premium received = 900 - 850 - 18 = 32p
Upside potential = difference in premiums = 35 - 17 = 18p
  = overall premium received
U/D ratio = 18/32 = 0.56

Table 11.2. Upside (U) and Downside (D) Potentials for September and December Glaxo Put Spreads. The Glaxo share price is 917p.

Expiry Date	Buy 850s/Sell 900s			Buy 850s/Sell 950s			Buy 900s/Sell 950s		
	U	D	U/D	U	D	U/D	U	D	U/D
September	18	32	0.56	41	59	0.69	23	27	0.85
December	19	31	0.61	46	54	0.85	27	23	1.17

Taking all six possible spreads, we get the values shown in Table 11.2. Broadly speaking, bull call spreads and bull put spreads are fairly similar in their risk reward patterns. There are two aspects that make put spreads slightly more attractive. Firstly, the difference in premiums between the two legs is actually pocketed at the time of the transaction, whereas with a call spread the investor has to pay this difference immediately. The second point is that the U/D ratios are higher than for the corresponding call spreads. This means that, in simple terms, the profit/loss situation is more favourable to the investor. Note that put spreads can be less attractive in another respect, and that is that they may be exercised against you at a point before you reach the maximum upside potential. This is particularly true if the written leg of the spread is well in-the-money.

SUBSEQUENT ACTION

If the Share Price Falls

The best action is simply to hold the position, since you already took into account this risk of the share price falling when you opened the position. Even if you are now totally convinced that the price will fall even further, any other action than holding will carry with it an even higher risk. For example, rolling down by closing out the original spread and opening a new spread with lower striking prices will simply lock in the loss that was made on the original spread. If you are not careful, you could end up by initiating a new spread whose potential for profit is not enough to cover the loss made on the original spread. The circumstance where you could take action is if you are convinced that the share price fall is only temporary, and that the price will shortly move up so strongly that it will outperform your original expectations. If you held a bull call spread, then closing the position on the written call will now leave you holding a straightforward call at what was originally a low striking price, but now, as a result of the price fall, is a well out-of-the-money option. The share price must move considerably higher if you are to make a profit, since of course the original loss must be wiped out. Quite obviously, changing the strategy from a spread to a call option position unavoidably takes on board substantially higher risk.

If the Share Price Rises

If the price rises in line with your original expectations, then continue to hold the spread. Only if you become convinced that a much larger rise is in prospect should you consider changing the original strategy for a more bullish one. If you have a bull call spread, one move is to close the written call position, leaving you holding a simple call position which is now, as a result of the price rise, heavily in-the-money. The profit you made on the original spread is now locked into this new position, and therefore is put at risk. The downside potential for this call is higher than that of the original spread, because heavily in-the-money options will lose value virtually on a penny for penny basis if the share price starts to move downwards again. A much better approach than closing the written call position is to roll the whole spread upwards.

Rolling Up

This is carried out by closing out the original bull spread and opening another one at higher striking prices. There is an additional risk involved, since the breakeven point is now higher, necessitating a higher share price rise than was the case with the original spread. The point can be illustrated by reference to Jaguar options on 4th December 1987. The investor opened a 280/300 bull call spread in the April options. The premiums were 22p and 19p respectively, so that the overall cost of the spread was 3p plus expenses. The share price at the time was 263p. The downside and upside potentials were:

Downside = difference in premiums = 22-19 = 3p paid
Upside = difference in striking prices - difference in premiums
= 300 - 280 - 3 = 17p

The maximum gain of this spread will be reached when the share price rises above the 300p striking price of the written option. By 15th December, with the share price at 299p, the spread was virtually at its maximum profit, and the investor became convinced that a further price rise was in the offing. He therefore closed the initial spread and opened the 300/330 spread. The premiums on 15th December were: 47, 36 and 23p for the April 280, 300 and 330 options respectively.

Thus, to close the initial spread:
Write 280 option @ 47p
Buy 300 option @ 36p
Amount received = 11p, i.e. a profit of 8p over the original 3p paid.

To open the new spread:
Buy 300 option @ 36p
Write 330 option @ 23p
Net outlay = 36 - 23 = 13p

The new downside potential is this 13p payed, but since the previous profit was 8p, the overall downside potential is therefore 5p.
The new upside potential is 330 - 300 -13 = 17p
Thus having pocketed the initial profit of 8p, there is now the potential to make a further 17p profit, making the overall profit 25p.

Note that additional risk has now been taken on board, since the share price has to rise above the highest striking price, i.e. higher than 330p from its current level of 299p before this maximum profit is made.

BEAR SPREADS

Bear spreads can be achieved by using the opposite transactions to those used in a bull spread. The two methods available are thus to buy a call with a high striking price and sell a call with a low striking price, or to buy a put with a high striking price and sell a put with a low striking price. Just as bull spreads

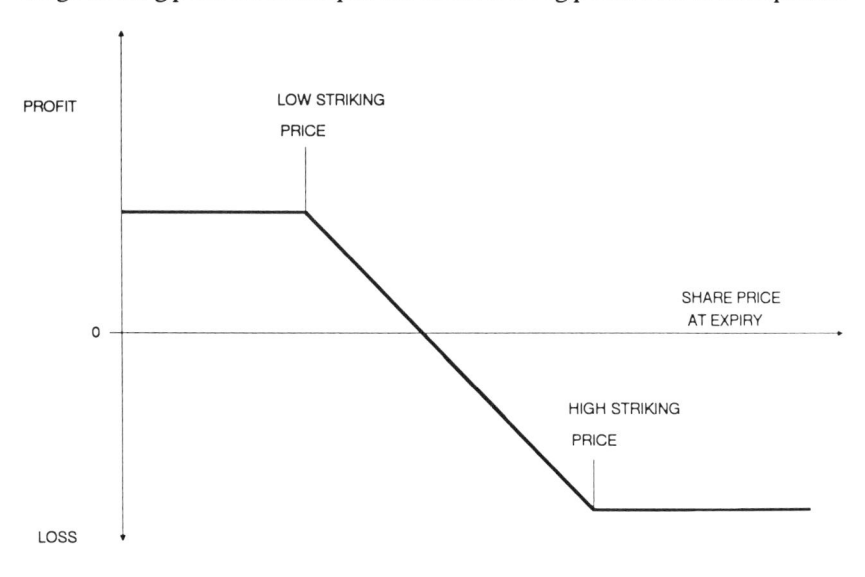

Figure 11.2. Profit and loss situation for a bear call spread at expiry.

were for those investors who were moderately bullish, then bear spreads are for those investors who are moderately bearish of the share price. Investors who are very bearish should use the simple strategies discussed in the earlier chapters.

Costs and Margin Requirement

If we ignore dealing costs, then the cost of a bear spread position is the difference between the two premiums. For a bear call spread, the higher striking price calls are of course less expensive than lower striking price calls, and therefore since the call spread is constructed by buying the high striking price call and selling the lower striking price call, the investor will be credited with the difference. Conversely, for a bear put spread, the higher striking price puts are higher priced than the lower striking price puts, and therefore the investor will have to pay the difference. There will be a margin requirement for the bear call spread which is calculated as the difference between the two striking prices less the net premium which has been credited. There is no margin requirement for bear put spreads.

BEAR CALL SPREADS

Gain/Loss Potential - Limited Gain, Limited Loss

The profit and loss position for a bear call spread at expiry time is shown in Figure 11.2. The maximum profit is equal to the difference in the two premiums, i.e. the net premium credited or received. The maximum loss is equal to the difference between the two striking prices minus the net premium received. The maximum return is obtained when the share price is below the lower of the two share prices.

The values for profit and loss will of course depend on the premiums and striking prices of the particular options which make up the spread, but for any bear call spread the overall shape of the graph will remain the same. We can take the example of Glaxo which was used to illustrate bull spreads and carry out the appropriate calculation of upside and downside potentials for the bear call spread:

Glaxo Share price: 917p
Call Option Premiums: June 850s, 73p; 900s, 30p; 950s, 7p
September 850s, 110p; 900s, 75p; 950s, 48p
December 850s, 120p; 900s, 88p; 950s, 62p

Ignoring the June options, since there are only a few weeks to go to expiry, it is possible to construct three September call spreads and three December call spreads out of this data:

1. Buy 950s, write 900s
2. Buy 950s, write 850s
3. Buy 900s, write 850s

As an example of the calculation for a Glaxo September Bear Call Spread, buying 950s @ 48p and writing 900s @ 75p:

Downside potential = high striking price - low striking price - net premium received
= 950 - 900 - 27 = 23p
Upside potential = difference in premiums
= 75 - 48 = 27p = overall premium received
U/D ratio = 27/23 = 1.17

162 TRADED OPTIONS SIMPLIFIED

Taking all six possible put spreads, we get the values shown in Table 11.3.

Table 11.3. Upside (U) and Downside (D) Potentials for September and December Glaxo Bear Call Spreads. The Glaxo share price is 917p.

Expiry Date	Buy 950s/Sell 900s			Buy 950s/Sell 850s			Buy 900s/Sell 850s		
	U	D	U/D	U	D	U/D	U	D	U/D
September	23	27	1.17	62	38	1.63	35	15	2.33
December	26	24	1.08	58	42	1.38	32	18	1.78

The least bearish investor will be looking at the 900/950 call spread, since with a share price of 917p, it is only necessary for a further fall in share price to below 900p for the spread to achieve its maximum profit. The two other spreads, using the 850 option, requires a 67p fall for maximum profit, although of course this profit is higher to compensate for the additional risk.

BEAR PUT SPREADS

Gain/Loss Potential - Limited Gain, Limited Loss

The profit/loss graph for a bear put spread at expiry is very much the same shape as that for a bear call spread as shown in Figure 11.2. The maximum gain is equal to the difference in the striking prices less the net premium which has been paid for the spread. The maximum loss is equal to the net premium which has been paid, i.e. the difference between the premium received for writing the lower striking price put and the premium paid for the higher striking price put.

For the same Glaxo example, the put data is as follows:

Glaxo Share Price: 917p

Put Option Premiums: June 850s, 1.5p; 900s, 10p; 950s, 38p
September 850s, 17p; 900s, 35p; 950s, 58p
December 850s, 29p; 900s, 48p; 950s, 75p

Ignoring the June options, since there are only a few weeks to go to expiry, it is possible to construct three September put spreads and three December put spreads out of this data:

1. Buy 950s, write 900s
2. Buy 950s, write 850s
3. Buy 900s, write 850s

As an example of the calculation for a Glaxo September put spread, buying 950s @ 58p and writing 900s @ 35p:

Downside potential = difference in premiums = 58 - 35 = 23p
Upside potential = high striking price - low striking price - net premium
received = 950 - 900 - 23 = 27p
U/D ratio = 18/32 = 0.85

Taking all six possible put spreads, we get the values shown in Table 11.4.

Table 11.4. Upside (U) and Downside (D) Potentials for September and December Glaxo Bear Call Spreads. The Glaxo share price is 917p.

Expiry Date	Buy 950s/Sell 900s			Buy 950s/Sell 850s			Buy 900s/Sell 850s		
	U	D	U/D	U	D	U/D	U	D	U/D
September	23	27	0.85	41	59	0.69	18	32	0.56
December	27	23	1.17	46	54	0.85	19	31	0.61

SUBSEQUENT ACTION

Share Price Rise

The best tactic in these circumstances is to continue to hold the existing position. The potential loss is already quantified and no further risk is being taken by staying put. Only if you feel that the price will continue to rise strongly should you contemplate any other course of action. Once such course of action is to close out one leg of the spread to leave a bought call position in the case of a bear call spread, or a written put position in the case of a bear put spread. You will then be left holding either a high striking price call, or a written position in a low striking price put. Note that both of these may have moved into an in-the-money situation as a result of the share price rise. There is quite an amount of risk associated with deep in-the-money options, since subsequent price movement may be on a penny for penny basis with the share price itself, so that erosion of their value will be extremely rapid with an adverse share price trend.

Share Price Fall

A tactic other than continuing to hold the position should be employed only if you are totally convinced that the share price will continue to fall over the time remaining to expiry. If you are holding a bear put spread, one tactic is to close the position on the written put, leaving you holding a simple put option position, at a striking price that is now deeply in-the-money as a result of the share price fall. As with the position discussed above, subsequent adverse share price movement will rapidly diminish the value of this option, making it a high risk holding. With a bear call spread, a corresponding tactic would be to close the position on the bought call, leaving a written call position, although this is not usually to be recommended in view of the low premiums associated with such calls, which gives them a low profit potential for the degree of risk involved. A much better alternative is to roll down the entire spread.

Rolling Down

This is carried out by closing out the current spread and opening a new one at lower striking prices. There is an increased risk involved, since the breakeven point is now lower, i.e. the share price has to fall much further than was the case with the original spread before the new position moves into profit. The possibilities are best illustrated by reference to Woolworth options on 20th November 1987. The share price was 287p, and the premiums for April call options were : 280s, 50p; 300s, 35p and 330s, 20p. An investor opened a 280/300 bear call spread by writing the 280s and buying the 300s, with the following potentials:
Upside potential = net premium received = 50 - 35 = 15p
Downside potential = 300 - 280 - 15 = 5p
U/D ratio = 3

By 11th December 1987, the share price had fallen to 261p, and the investor, certain that a further fall was imminent, decided to stay on for the ride by agressively rolling down to the 240/280 spread. The premiums for the April options were: 240s, 45; 260s, 35; 280s, 25; 300s, 14 and 330s, 4p.
To close the previous position, the steps are:
Write the 300 option, premium received = 14p
Buy the 280 option, premium payed = 25p
Net outlay = 11p
Since an initial premium of 15p was received, the net profit = 4p, less of course dealing expenses.

To open the new position:
Write the 240 option, premium received = 45p
Buy the 280 option, premium payed = 25p
Net premium received = 20p
Upside potential = net premium received = 20p
Downside potential = 280 -240 - 20 = 20p
The investor now has the potential to add a further 20p to the profit of 4p already received. Note that this maximum potential is only realised if the share price falls below 240p, and therefore the investor is operating at higher risk than in his initial position.

CALENDAR SPREADS

Although calendar spreads can be constructed so as to be bullish, bearish or neutral strategies, they are mostly used by investors who have neutral expectations for the share price. A neutral calendar spread will use options that are close to being at-the- money. In-the-money options should be avoided because of the risk that the written leg is exercised against the writer, thereby destroying the basis of the strategy.

The strategy involves the writing of a near expiry option and the purchase of a further expiry option. Although either puts or calls can be used, the time values of call options are usually somewhat higher than those of put options. Large time values for the written option makes the calendar spread particularly attractive, and so only call options are considered in this discussion. Before illustrating the profit/loss situation for calendar spreads by means of a diagram, it is useful to discuss the basic features that the investor should be looking for before taking his decision on the best calendar spread for the particular circumstances. Taking data already presented earlier, that given in Table 7.2 in Chapter 7 for Dixons, several calendar spreads could be constructed out of the 180 options on 12th February 1988. The premiums for the three options were:

March 180s, 12p; June 180s, 20p; September 180s, 28p; share price 180p.

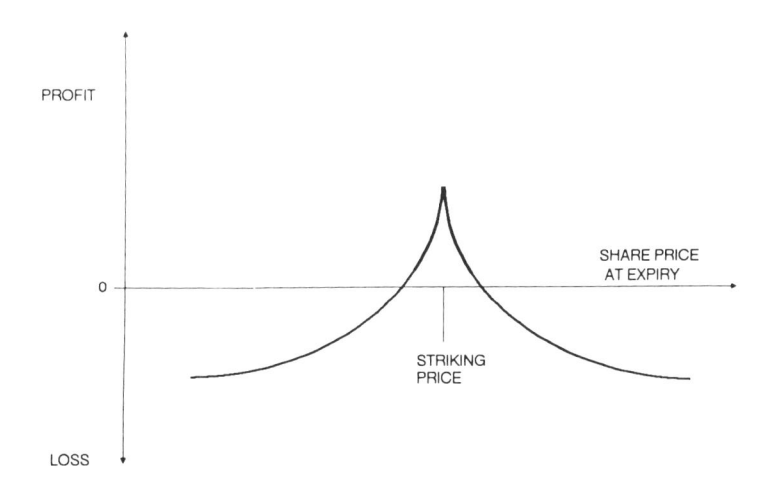

Figure 11.3. Profit and loss situation for a calendar spread at expiry.

The three calendar spreads possible from these options are:

1. Write the March 180s, buy June 180s
2. Write the March 180s, buy September 180s
3. Write June 180s, buy September 180s

Ignoring the dealing costs and the spread of premiums between buying and writing the same options, the outlays for these three calendar spreads are:

Spread 1: receive 12p for March 180s pay 20p for June 180s net outlay, i.e. maximum loss: 8p

Spread 2: receive 12p for March 180s pay 28p for September 180s net outlay, i.e. maximum loss: 16p

Spread 3: receive 20p for June 180s pay 28p for September 180s net outlay, i.e. maximum loss: 8p

The simplest way of deciding between these three possibilities is to look at each leg of the spread independently, i.e. the best approach to the written leg and the best approach to the purchased leg.

As discussed in Chapter 8, time is to the disadvantage of the option writer, since a trend that initially is moving in the right direction may well reverse this direction within the timescale of a longer expiry option. Although there are sometimes good reasons to ignore this fact, for example the discovery that an option has an anomalously high premium, these should not be allowed to influence the situation with a calendar spread. Applying this principle to the three possibilities above, we would rule out strategy 3. For the near expiry option, the objective is to find options with high time values, i.e. high CPP values, since these will reduce the overall cost of the spread. Since we are also looking for these to deteriorate as rapidly as possible, the ideal time is when there are about six weeks left to expiry, and the option has just started on its downward decay, as illustrated for example by Figure 5.4 in Chapter 5.

Out of the remaining two spreads we are faced with a simple choice - 8p downside potential for the medium expiry June option or 16p downside potential for the longer expiry September option. This time, the advantage lies with the longer expiry option, since as has been pointed out, there is more time for an adverse trend to rectify itself before expiry of the option. The only question is whether this advantage is worth the additional 8p per spread. Aspects such as CPP values, etc. as discussed in Chapter 7 should be taken into account before making the final decision. As always, the investor should be fairly clear as to the future direction of the share price from techniques such as channel analysis.

Loss/Gain Potential - Limited Loss, Limited Gain

The potential for gain and loss has to be evaluated for the complete spread prior to the expiration of the written leg of the spread, since after this point, the investor is left simply with a call option position. Because of this, the ideal combination to use, but which may be difficult to find, will be options where the CPPs are high for the near expiry and low for the further expiry, and where the projected share price movement is sideways until the written option expires, and then sharply upwards in order to maximise the profit from the remaining leg.

The profit/loss potential for a calendar call spread is shown in Figure 11.3. The maximum loss occurs when the share price falls or rises below or above a share price band whose limits unfortunately cannot be calculated in advance. This is because these limits depend upon time values which of course cannot be predicted. However the extent of the maximum loss is known, and this is the net outlay which has been made for the spread. As far as the maximum profit is concerned, again this cannot be quantified since we cannot predict the time values which might apply to the far option at the time of expiry of the near option. We can though say at which share price the profit will be at its maximum, and that price is the striking price of the furthest option of the spread. This is because as has been stated previously, time values are at their highest for at-the-money options, so that for maximum profit the furthest option should be standing at-the-money.

SUBSEQUENT ACTION

Naturally if the share price behaviour you anticipated when you opened the spread is maintained, then you need do nothing more than leave the position as it is until expiry. Unlike the previous spreads in which the options all expired at the same time, with a calendar spread the first leg expires ahead of the second leg. At expiry of the first leg therefore you are left holding a call option with at least three months to go until expiry. This follow-on position would require you to have bullish expectations for the share price as opposed to the neutral expectations that you had when you opened the spread. You may of course have changed you view to a more bullish one, and if so should maintain your position of holding this call option. If your further expectations are for a continuing neutral share price, i.e. you have not changed your original stance, or if you now think the share price will fall, then you should close this second leg of the calendar spread, since otherwise your investment is not making further profit.

If the Share Price Falls

The action you should take following a share price fall depends upon whether you think the price fall will continue, the share price will stay neutral at its lower level, or will reverse direction and rise. If you think the fall will continue, then probably the best tactic is to liquidate the position, especially if this gives you a small profit. If you can see a fall to a lower level which you expect to remain stable, then you can roll down the option.

If you think the share price is now stable at a lower level, then the best tactic is to roll down.

If you think the share price will reverse direction and start to rise, then you can either close out the entire spread, hopefully still making a profit, or you can increase your profit potential by closing out the nearby written call, leaving yourself holding a further expiry call option, which of course is then the stance for a bullish investor, as discussed in Chapter 7. This will give you an unlimited profit potential, although of course since you will almost certainly be standing at a loss on the original position because of the costs of closing the written call the share price will have to rise a reasonable amount before you move into profit.

Rolling Down

This is the tactic to pursue if the price has fallen and you think the price will stabilise at this level, or you can anticipate a lower level at which the price will stabilise. Since we stated earlier that the maximum profit will be achieved if the spread expires in an at-the-money situation, then the striking prices for the rolled down spread should be close to the price level at which you think the position will stabilise.

If we assume that an investor thinks the Dixons share price will fall from 180p to about 160p and then stabilise, then the steps required to close the original position and roll down are:

Buy the near expiry March 180 option
Sell the further expiry June 180 option
Write the March 160 option
Buy the June 160 option

The investor may be in the fortunate position of making at least a small profit on the original spread after all expenses, and will then have the opportunity of making a further profit on the rolled-down spread.

If the Share Price Rises

Action here depends upon whether you think the share price will continue to rise, will stay stable at a higher level, or will reverse direction and fall.

If you think the share price will continue to rise, then you can either close out the entire position, hopefully with a profit or alternatively you can close the written leg of the spread, leaving yourself with a further expiry call option, which of course is the stance that a bullish investor would have adopted in any case.

If you think the share price will fall back, then it is probably sensible to continue to hold the position, so that it will move back towards the maximum profit position. An alternative if you now become more bearish is to adopt the stance which the bears would have had, i.e. to hold a written call position. This is of course achieved by closing the further expiry bought leg of the option, leaving you with the shorter expiry written option.

If you think the share price will stabilise at a higher level, then the best tactic is to roll up the spread.

Rolling Up

This is the tactic to pursue if the price has risen and you think the price will stabilise at this level, or you can anticipate a higher level at which the price will stabilise. Since we stated earlier that the maximum profit will be achieved if the spread expires in an at-the-money situation, then the striking prices for the rolled up spread should be close to the price level at which you think the position will stabilise.

Using the Dixons case as an example, if we assume that an investor thinks the Dixons share price will rise from 180p to about 200p and then stabilise, then the steps required to close the original position and roll up are:

Buy the near expiry March 180 option
Sell the further expiry June 180 option
Write the March 200 option
Buy the June 200 option

The investor is now in the position of having the potential for further profit from this new spread, and may also have made a small profit on the original spread, depending on how far the price rise had gone before the decision to roll up was taken.

BUTTERFLY SPREADS

Butterfly spreads are strategies for those investors who have neutral expectation for the share price. Unlike the previous spreads which used only two legs, the butterfly spread has three components to it. Although puts can be used, calls have an advantage, and the butterfly is initiated by buying a call with a low striking price, writing two calls with middle striking prices and buying a call with a high striking price. The striking prices are normally chosen so as to be equally spaced, and for a neutral strategy, the middle striking price should be as close as possible to the share price. Naturally, one consequence of having so many legs to the strategy is that the dealing expenses will be higher than those for bull, bear or calendar spreads. The newcomer to traded options should avoid butterfly spreads until he has become experienced in all other traded option strategies, because it is often easy to open a butterfly where the chance of profit is extremely low.

Costs and Margin Requirements

If the butterfly is looked at as a combination of a bull call spread and a bear call spread, then the margin required by the butterfly is the margin that would be required by the bear spread half of the strategy, i.e. the difference between the two striking prices involved in this bear spread part.

Gain-Loss Potential - Limited Gain, Limited Loss

The maximum loss which can be sustained in a butterfly is the difference (a net debit) between the premiums paid for the bought options and the premiums received for the two written contracts, plus of course the expenses involved in the overall transaction. The maximum gain is obtained when the share price is at the middle striking price, and the profit is equal to the difference between two adjacent striking prices and the original outlay. The situation is shown graphically in Figure 11.4. Since the profit is dependent upon

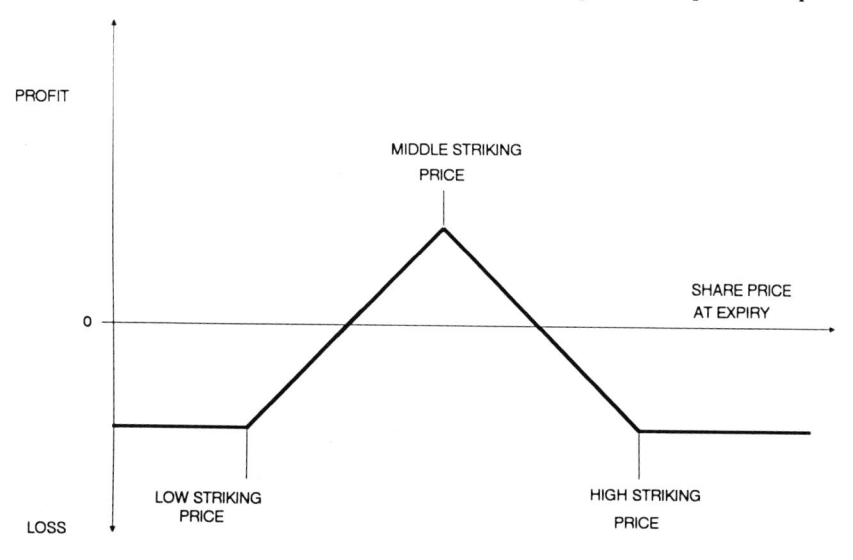

Figure 11.4. Profit and loss situation for a butterfly spread at expiry.

the spacing of the striking prices, obviously this profit is maximised if the striking prices can be chosen so as to be as far apart as possible. In the early life of options this is not possible due to the restricted number of striking prices available. The profit is also crucially dependent on the costs of the transactions, since the spread consists of three such transactions. The procedures used in identifying underpriced options by means of CPP values should be employed for the bought options, while the same procedures should be used to identify overpriced options for the written leg of the strategy. By this means the overall cost of the spread will be minimised. Adopting any other policy than this will make it a difficult strategy out of which to make any considerable profit.

SUBSEQUENT ACTION

Obviously if the share price stays more or less static at a similar level to the middle striking price, then the spread is achieving its objective, and no action needs to be taken. If the share price is falling or rising then action does need to be taken. This action of course will depend upon how you see the share price behaving after the current movement, i.e. will it reverse direction or continue in the same trend. One tactic that is usually not applicable to a butterfly is to roll down or roll up. This is because of the higher costs of closing and reopening the new positions in so many option series. It is possible that where you expect the share price to stabilise at a new lower or a new higher position there may just be a glimmer of a profit in such a tactic, but it has to be looked at most closely before taking such action. A key to understanding how to deal with an adverse share price movement when holding a butterfly spread is to consider that the spread is simply composed of two other spreads - a bear call spread made from the bought high striking price option and one of the written medium striking price options, and a bull spread made from the bought low striking price option and the other written medium striking price option. Thus by closing out the appropriate half of the butterfly, the investor can be left holding either a bull call spread or a bear call spread, depending upon whether he thinks the share price will continue to rise if it is currently rising or will continue to fall if it is currently falling. If you think the present adverse trend will stabilise into a static share price which is higher or lower than you first anticipated, then provided this static share price is within the profit band for the spread, the best tactic is to continue to hold the position.

If the Share Price Rises

As we have mentioned, one tactic is to close out half of the spread, leaving a bull call spread in existence. To do this, the steps are:

Write the high striking price option
Buy one medium striking price option

This approach is the best if you have now changed to being moderately bullish for the share price. If you have become even more bullish of the share price, then you have another route available. This is to close out three of the four options, leaving you simply holding either the low striking price call option which is now even further in the money or the high striking price call which may or may not have moved to an in-the-money position as a result of the share price rise.

If the Share price falls

As mentioned earlier, one tactic is to close out half of the spread, leaving a bear call spread in existence. The steps are:
Write the low striking price option
Buy one medium striking price option

This approach is best if you have now changed to being moderately bearish for the share price. If you feel even more bearish, then an alternative route available is to close out the bought high and low striking price options and perhaps one of the medium striking price options, leaving either one or two of the written calls in place.

CHAPTER 12

Advanced Strategies. 2. Straddles and Combinations

The advanced strategies discussed in the last Chapter had one aspect in common - they involved either all call options or all put options, even though these may have had different striking prices or even different expiry dates. There is another way in which an option strategy can be built up, and that is by the use of both a call and a put at the same time. These strategies fall into two categories - straddles and combinations. Straddles are a restricted version of combinations in which the investor buys a put and a call option (buying a straddle) or writes a put and a call option (writing a straddle) with identical expiry dates and striking prices. In combinations, anything goes - it is possible to mix both expiry dates and striking prices, although the investor is still in the position of either buying the appropriate put and call or writing the appropriate put and call.

STRADDLES

Buying a Straddle

Here the investor buys a put and a call option on the same share, with both options having the same expiry date and the same exercise price. The straddle buyer is expecting the share price to move and not stay neutral, but the unusual aspect of the strategy is that the direction of the share price movement is immaterial. The straddle buyer will profit if the share price moves either upwards or downwards. This price movement has to be of a reasonable extent since the two option premiums will have been payed.

Profit/Loss Potential - Unlimited Profit, Limited Loss

The graphical representation of the profit and loss situation is shown in Figure 12.1. The maximum loss which can be incurred is the sum of the two premiums payed, plus of course the expenses involved in the transactions. The point of maximum loss is where the share price expires at the striking price of the straddle, i.e. where there has been no movement in the share price since the straddle was opened. The maximum profit is virtually unlimited, since the

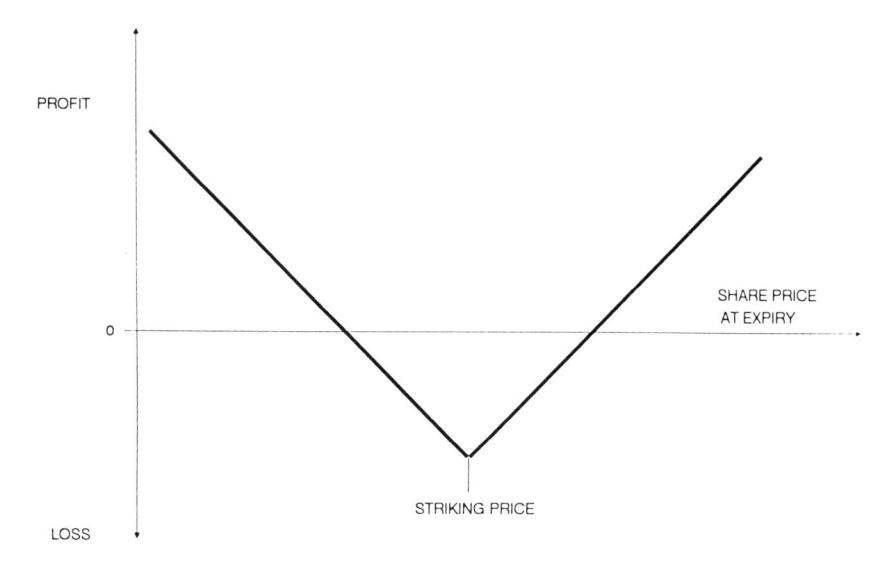

Figure 12.1. Profit and loss situation for a bought straddle at expiry.

share price can either drop to zero, or can rise to an infinite level, although of course the original total premium payed and expenses have to be taken into consideration.

SUBSEQUENT ACTION

If the Share Price Rises

This is one of the outcomes that makes the straddle profitable, and therefore if you consider that the price rise will continue, then the only sensible course is to continue to hold the straddle. If you think the share price rise may reverse, so bringing you back below the breakeven point into a potential loss situation, then the best tactic is to close the position, taking the existing profit even though it may be smaller than you originally expected.

If the Share Price Falls

The same comment applies here as for a price rise. The strategy is working, so stay with it unless you feel the price fall may reverse, so eroding the profit that has accrued so far. The sensible course in this situation is to close the position, taking the existing profit.

If the Share Price Remains Static

This of course is exactly the outcome that you do not want, since the profit in a straddle depends on price movement away from the original striking price at which the straddle was initiated. You can grin and bear it in the hope that a price movement will occur before the rapidly nearing expiry date, but of course the premiums of both the put and the call will be falling as a result of the disappearing time values. It is best to close out the position if you become convinced that no further movement will occur, so that you retrieve at least some of the premium still remaining in both options.

Writing a Straddle

This is the opposite strategy to that employed by the straddle purchaser, and therefore the writer expects the opposite outcome, i.e. expects that the share price will remain static.

Profit/Loss Potential - Limited Profit, Unlimited Loss

The profit and loss situation for a written straddle is shown in Figure 12.1. Since the straddle writer has written both a put and a call option, he will receive a premium from both these transactions. This premium, less of course the expenses of the transactions, is the maximum profit that the straddle writer receives, and he will keep this if the share price stays within a short distance either side of the option striking price. Since the share price rise is unlimited,

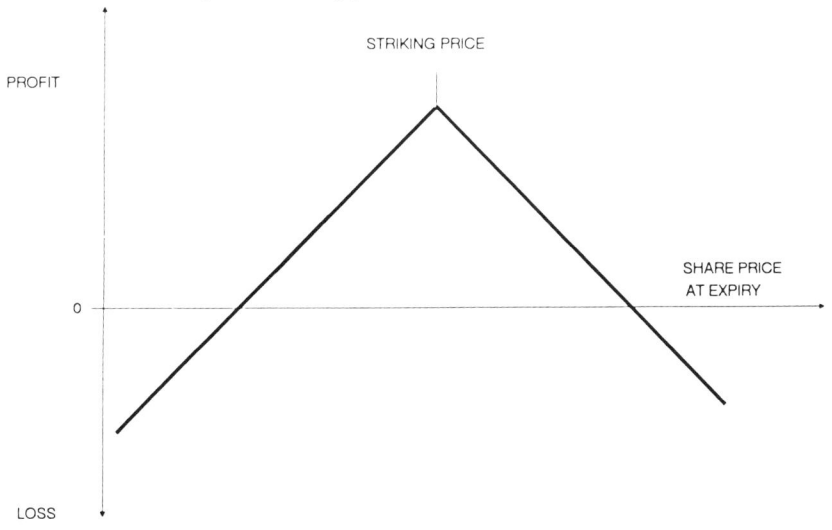

Figure 12.2. Profit and loss situation for a written straddle at expiry.

he may have the written call option exercised against him and have to pay this unlimited price to deliver the shares. Conversely, if the share price falls virtually to zero, he will have to buy the shares from the buyer of the put who will be exercising against him.

Margin Requirements for Written Straddle

In this case, the writer will have to deposit a margin equivalent to 25% of the share price, plus an adjustment for the degree to which the put and call lies in-the-money. Naturally, since the share price will be constantly changing, then with a continually rising or falling share price, there will be constant calls to increase the margin. Because of the unlimited nature of the risk in a written straddle position, it should not be considered unless the writer is covered by holding the underlying shares.

SUBSEQUENT ACTION

If the Share Price Remains Static

As a writer you should continue to hold the position, since everything is proceeding according to plan. Only if you develop a feeling that this situation cannot last any longer should you take action. You then have the possibility of closing the position, which as a result of the static price so far should have seen premiums lose time value and thus give you a small profit on closing. If you feel you know which direction the share price will start to move, then you can close one half of the straddle, leaving a written call if you think prices will fall, or a written put if you think prices will rise.

If the Share Price Rises

If you are convinced, and only if you are convinced, that the rise is temporary and that the share price will fall back again, then continue to hold the position, since it will move back into profit. If you feel the rise will continue, then there are two courses of action - close out the whole position, taking either a small profit or a small loss, or close out the written call position, leaving you with a written put. This will reduce the risk of loss, although the profit potential will also be small.

If the Share Price Falls

As with a rising share price, you should maintain the position only if you are very convinced that the price fall is only temporary, and that the position will soon move back into profit. In any other circumstance you have two possibilities - either close out the whole straddle, possibly still with a small profit, or close out the written put position, leaving you with a written call. Again, this reduces the risk of loss, although the profit potential is small.

COMBINATIONS

Because of the variety of combinations possible, it is possible in a book of this nature to cover only the fundamentals of such strategies. The more usual combinations used are where the put and the call are both out-of-the-money and both are either bought or written. Both the bought and written out-of-the-money combinations would have the striking price of the call above the current share price and the striking price of the put below the current share price.

Bought Out-of-the-Money Combination

This is the strategy for an investor who expects share price movement, but is not sure in which direction this will occur.

Profit/Loss Potential - Unlimited Profit, Limited Loss

The profit and loss situation for this strategy is shown in Figure 12.3. The maximum loss is the total premium paid, and the loss does not start to decrease until the share price moves outside of either of the two share prices.

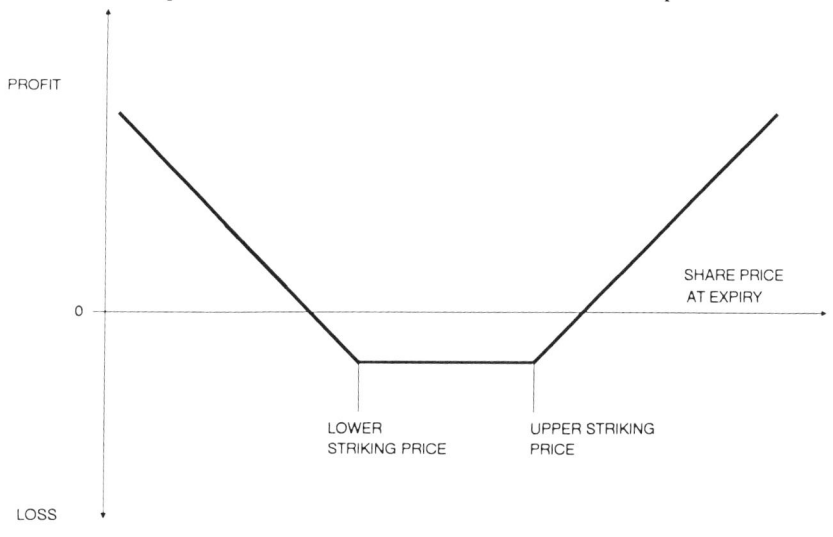

Figure 12.3. Profit and loss situation for a bought out-of-the-money combination at expiry.

SUBSEQUENT ACTION

It is best to follow the same tactics as for a bought straddle, since the general principles are the same. If the share price is falling or rising, then leave the position as it is, since everything is then going to plan.

Written Out-of-the-Money Combination

This is the strategy for the investor who expects the share price to remain more or less static between the two striking prices.

Profit/Loss Potential - Limited Profit, Unlimited Loss

The profit and loss situation for this strategy is shown in Figure 12.4. The maximum profit is the sum of the two premiums received for writing each of the two options, less of course the expenses of the transactions. The profit does

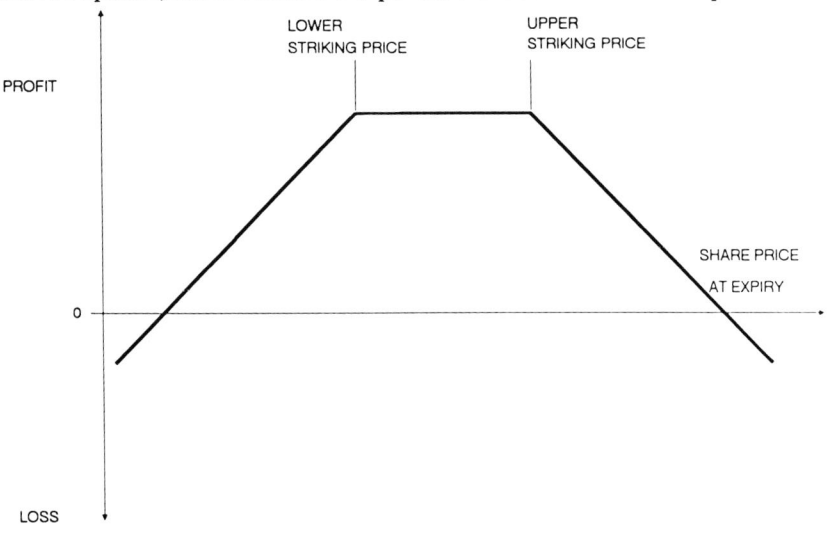

Figure 12.4. Profit and loss situation for a written out-of-the-money combination at expiry.

not start to decrease until the share price moves outside of the upper or lower striking price.

SUBSEQUENT ACTION

Because of the unlimited nature of the loss with a written combination, it is important that action is taken at the first sign that the share price is moving away from the band between the two striking prices. The general tactics in such a situation are the same as those discussed above for written straddles.